GOD'S GRACE AND MERCY

JESUS PRAYED FOR ALL WHO WOULD FOLLOW HIM
JOHN 17:11

REVEREND J. A. JEFFERSON

October 30, 2011

AuthorHouse™ LLC
1663 Liberty Drive
Bloomington, IN 47403
www.authorhouse.com
Phone: 1-800-839-8640

Published by AuthorHouse   03/20/2014

ISBN: 978-1-4918-1277-8 (sc)
ISBN: 978-1-4918-1278-5 (e)

PREFACE

BY THE GRACE OF GOD THROUGH OUR LORD JESUS CHRIST

Jesus prayed for all who would follow Him, including you and others you know. He prayed for unity (John 17:11), protection from the evil one (John 17:17), knowing that Jesus prayed for us should give us confidence as we work for His kingdom.

Jesus prayed for unity among the believers based on the believers' unity with him and the Father. Christians can know unity among themselves if they are living in union with God. Each branch living in union with the vine is united with all other branches doing the same (John 17:21-23).

PRAYING CHRIST'S PRAYER AGENDA

Neither pray for these alone, but for them also which shall believe on me through their word; that they all may be one, as you Father are in me, and I in you, that they also may be one in us. That the world may believe that you have sent me (John 17:20-21).

I'M SO GRATEFUL FOR WHAT YOU HAVE DONE

I'm so grateful for what you've done and so glad that you are you! You've made a difference in my life. It is a joyful and pleasant thing to be thankful.

Be careful for nothing; but in everything by prayer and supplication with thanksgiving; take no thought for your life; what you shall eat, or drink. Humble yourselves therefore under the mighty Hand of God, that he may exalt you in due time, casting all your care upon him; for he cares for you (1-Peter 5:6,7).

In everything give thanks, for this is the will of God In Christ Jesus concerning you (1-Thessalonians 5:18)

Happy Thanksgiving:

Chaplain J. A. Jefferson
jj2558@bellsouth.net
864-221-9144

TABLE OF CONTENTS

THE BEST CHRISTMAS EVER

The best Christmas you could ever have is when someone loves you in spite of rather than because of. When you love someone because of, it usually involve emotions. When emotions are in involved it brings us to the attention of a deed rather than in spite of.

When love is given because the person has done something which caused you to love them for what they have done, what if that person hasn't given you anything? Would you or could you still love that person in spite of rather than because of?

What have we done to earn God's love? Is His love because of or is it in spite of? The only time in creation we see the emotions of God are when He looked and saw the evil of His creation. The thoughts of mankind's heart was only evil continually and it grieved God to His heart that He made man on the earth. This showed emotions, but He still loved mankind in spite of rather than because of (Genesis 6: 5, 6; and John 3:16).

God so loved the world that He gave His only begotten Son, that whosoever believes in Him should not perish, but have everlasting life; For he whom God has sent speaks the words of God: for God gave not the Spirit by measure unto him, The Father loves the Son, and has given all things into his hand; He who believes on the Son has everlasting life: and he who believes not the Son shall not see life but the Wrath of God abide on him (John 3:34-36).

Although God said let us make man in our image and likeness and man became strangers and foreigners to God, He wants him back. That's the reason this is the best Christmas ever. He sent his only Son into the world to get back that which is His that He created in the beginning.

SENDING A SPECIAL WISH FOR A WONDERFUL HOLIDAY SEASON

CHAPLAIN J.A.JEFFERSON

jj2558@bellsouth.net
864-221-9144

INTRODUCTION TO SALVATION

SALVATION

In this section of the instruction of salvation I would like to point out the church in a way of working out your own salvation," in light of exhortation to unity, which means that the entire church is to work together to rid themselves of divisions and discord.

Wherefore, my beloved, as you have always obeyed, not as in my presence only, but now much more in my absence, work out your own salvation with fear and trembling (Philippians 2:12).

We must be careful about what we believe and how we live, especially when we are on our own. In the absence of Christian leaders, we must focus our attention and devotion even more on Christ so that we won't be sidetracked. As I have said many times before, the salvation that comes through Christ is described in these three different ways of seeing him: past, present, and future. Working out your own salvation is being all you can be according to the will of God through our Lord Jesus Christ until He returns.

Keeping in mind we are also in the process of being saved from the power of sin, we who are baptized into His death, burial and resurrection are crucified with Him according to Galatians 2:20. As Romans 8:13 states, *if you live after the flesh, you shall die: but if you through the Spirit do mortify the deeds of the body, you shall live.*

The "body" means to regard it as being dead the power of sin that's in the body (Romans 6:11). And (Galatians 5:24) when we regard sin's appeal as being dead and lifeless, we can ignore temptation when it comes. God has promised to give or make a way that we can escape our temptations, because there is no temptation that we will be faced with such is common to man (l-Corinthians 10:13).

REFLECTIONS

THIS BOOK CONTINUES THE REFLECTIONS ON THE WAY OF LIFE THROUGH THE WORDS OF THE HOLY BIBLE

There are sixty-six books and letters that make up the Bible. These are divided into chapters and verses that help make it easy reference. When Scriptures are quoted in passages they are written to refer to or mention by the way of example, or proof in publication, the first number after the name indicates the chapter of the Bible book or letter, and the next refers to the verse. For example, when the Scripture refers to "(2-Timothy 3:16)" means the second letter to Timothy, chapter 3, verse 16.

You will quickly become familiar with the Bible by looking up Scriptures passages. This book will help you understand the Bible much better then you could ever believe. You have in this book study and reflection in a way you will have to read the Bible to get some of the answers; I must say it is a great privilege having you as one of the most valuable readers of this book. I am sure you will enjoy and receive a blessing in reading as you apply the Word of God to growth in your life. Applying the teachings of the Bible requires some adjustments in the value of the life you live.

I wanted to be absolutely sure you received this valuable information concerning the way of life through the teachings of the word of the truth as it was given to me to share with you the salvation of God through Christ Jesus. The entire gospel comes to a focus in John 3: 16. It shows that God's love is not static or self-centered; it reaches out and draws others in. God sets the pattern of true love, the basis for all love relationships when you love someone dearly; you are willing to give freely to the point of self-sacrifice. I urge you to also read John 17:20-21.

SALVATION THROUGH CHRIST JESUS (JOHN 3:16)

Everlasting with God: The blessedness of the righteous, at last. Let us see what will be the end of God's poor despised people. Preferment: There have been times the iniquity of which has been such that men's piety has hindered their preferment in this world, and put them quite out of the way of raising estates; but those who keep God's way may be assured that in due time He will exalt them, to inherit the land. Read Psalm 37:34.

The Salvation of the Lord: *But the salvation of the righteous is of the Lord: He is their strength in the time of trouble* (Psalm 37:39).

God So Loved the World: *God so loved the world that he gave his only begotten son* through atonement (John 3:16; Leviticus 25:9). The entire gospel comes to a focus in this verse. God's love is not static or self-centered. It reaches out and draws others in. God sets the pattern of true love, the basis for all love relationships when you love someone dearly, you are willing to give freely to the point of self-sacrifice. God paid daily with the life of his Son, which is the highest price He could pay. Jesus accepted our punishment, by paying the price with His life for our sins, And then offered us the new life that He had bought for us.

When we share the gospel with others, our love must be like Jesus willingly giving up our own comfort and security so that others might join us in receiving God's love. Some people are repulsed by the idea of eternal life because their lives are miserable; but eternal life is not an extension of a person's miserable, mortal life. Eternal life is God's life embodied in Christ given to all that believe as a guarantee that they will live forever.

In eternal life there is no death, sickness, enemy, evil, or sin. When a person doesn't have Christ, he or she makes a choice as though this life is all he or she has. In reality, this life is just the introduction to the eternal. Receive this new life by faith and begin to enjoy all that happens from an eternal perspective.

To "Believe:" To "believe" is more than agreement that Jesus is God. It means to put our trust and confidence in Him that He alone can save us. It is to put Christ in charge of our present plans and eternal destiny. Believing is both trusting His words as reliable, and relying on Him for the power to change. If we have never trusted Christ, let this promise of everlasting life be yours and live. The reason is that God gave His only begotten Son because He loved us that much.

For God so loved the world, that he gave his only begotten Son, that whosoever believe in Him should not perish, but have everlasting life (John 3:16).

<u>The Year of Jubilee</u>: The year of jubilee was meant to be celebrated every (fifty) 50 years. It included canceling all debts, freeing all slaves, and returning to its original owners all land that had been sold.

There seem to be no indication in the Bible that the Year of Jubilee was ever carried out. If Israel had followed this practice faithfully, they would have been a society without permanent experience of the fifty 50 years Jubilee.

Then shall you cause the trumpet of the jubilee to sound on the tenth day of the seventh month, In the Day of Atonement shall you make the trumpet sound through all your land (Leviticus 25:9)

<u>Wait on the Lord</u>: It is difficult to wait patiently for God to act when we want change right away, but God promises that if we submit to His timing, He will honor us. Peter said, *Humble yourselves, therefore, under God's mighty hand, that he may lift you up in due time* (1-Peter 5:6).

Be patient, steadily doing the work God has given you to do, and allow God to choose the best time to change your circumstances.

Wait on the Lord, and keep his way, and he exalt you to inherit the land: when the wicked are cut off, you shall see it (Psalm 37:34).

We often worry about our position and status, hoping to get proper recognition for what we do but Peter advises us to remember that God's recognition counts more than human praise. God is able and willing to bless us according to His timing. Humbly obey God regardless of present circumstances and in His good time either in this life or in the next He will lift you up.

<u>Life Application of Peter</u>: Peter begins by thanking God for salvation (1-Peter 1:2-6). He explains to his readers that trials will refine their faith in (1-Peter 1:7-9). They should believe in spite of their circumstances, for many in past ages believed in God's plan of salvation, even the prophets of old who wrote about it but didn't understand it. But now salvation has been revealed in Christ. Read 1-Peter 1:10-13.

THE DAY OF ATONEMENT (Exodus 30:10)

The Viewpoint of the Coming Jesus: The coming of Christ Jesus was through the view point of the Old Testament prophetic concerning the Atone for sin.

This annual ceremony was called the Day of Atonement. On this day a sacrifice was made for the sins of the entire Israelite nation. This was the only day the high priest could enter the Most Holy Place, the innermost room of the tabernacle, where he asks God to forgive the people.

The Day of Atonement served as a reminder that the daily, weekly, and monthly sacrifices could cover sins only temporarily. It pointed toward Jesus Christ, the perfect atonement, who could remove sins forever.

Sin Offering of Atonements: *And Aaron shall make Atonement upon the horns of it once in a year with the blood of the sin offering of atonements: once in the year shall he make atonement upon it throughout your generation: it is most holy unto the Lord* (Exodus 30:10).

Divine Fellowship with Christ: Fellowship with Christ Jesus is found in Spiritual assemblies. *For where two or three are gathered together in my name, There am I in the midst of them* (Matthew 18:20).

Jesus Looked Ahead to a New Day: Jesus looked ahead to a new day when He would be present with His followers not in body but through His Holy Spirit. In the body of believers (the church), (read Ephesians 2:19-22) who is a holy temper in the Lord build upon the foundation of the apostles and prophets, Jesus Christ himself being the chief corner stone.

The sincere agreement of two people is more powerful than the superficial agreement of thousands, because Christ's Holy Spirit is with them. When two or more believers filled with the Holy Spirit will pray according to God's will their requests will be granted.

Who Gave Himself a Ransom (1-Timothy 2:6)

A Ransom for Our Sin: We as human beings are separated from God by sin, and only one person in the universe is holy enough to be our mediator and can stand between us and God and bring us together again (1-Timothy 2:5-6).

Jesus Is Both God and Man: *Jesus, who is both God and man, Jesus' sacrifice brought new life to all people. Jesus gave his life as a ransom for our sin* (Mark 10:45).

Jesus Understood the Law

Jesus understood the law well enough to quote Deuteronomy 6:5 and Leviticus 19:18. He correctly understood that the law demanded total devotion to God and love for one's neighbor. Jesus talked more about these laws elsewhere in the Bible, such as Matthew 19:16-22 and Mark 10:17-22.

<u>Principles for Loving Our Neighbor</u>: In Mark 10:37, we learn from the parable three principles about loving our neighbor.

1.   Lack of love is often easy to justify, even though it is never right.
2.   Our neighbor is anyone of any race, creed, or social background who is in need.
3.   Love means acting to meet the person's needs.

And he said, He who showed mercy on him. Then said Jesus unto him, **Go, and do you likewise** *(Luke 10:37).*

Differences Between Jews and Samaritans

There was deep hatred between Jews and the Samaritans. The Jews saw themselves as pure descendants of Abraham, while the Samaritans were a mixed race produced when Jews from the northern kingdom intermarried with other people after Israel's exile.

To this law the person least likely to act correctly would be the Samaritan. In fact, he could not bear to say "Samaritan" in answer to Jesus' question. This "expert's" attitude betrayed his lack of the very thing that he had earlier said the law commanded love.

But a certain Samaritan, as he journeyed, came where he was: and when he saw him, he had compassion on him (Luke 10:33).

A Collection of Attitudes

*   To the expert in the law, the wounded man was a subject to discuss.
*   To the robbers, the wounded man was someone to use and exploit.
*   To the righteous man, the wounded man was a problem to be avoided.
*   To the innkeeper, the wounded man was human being worth being cared and loved.
*   To Jesus, all of them and all of us were worth dying for.

Confronting the need of others brings out various attitudes in us. Jesus used the strong of the good but despised Samaritan to make clear what attitude was acceptable to Him. If we are honest, we often times will find ourselves in the place of the expert, in other words, we would be very skillful; having the training of Jesus Christ in the knowledge in some spiritual skill of love, it seems that we need to learn again who our neighbor is. Note these different attitudes toward the wounded men.

Justification Through Christ (Romans 4:25)

When we believe, an exchange takes place. We give Christ ourselves, and He gives us His righteousness and forgiveness, according to (2-Corinthians 5:25). There is nothing we can do to earn this. Only through Christ can we receive God's righteousness. What an incredible bargain this is for us! But sadly, many still choose to pass up this gift to continue "enjoying" their sin.

Who was delivered for our offences, and Was raised for our justification (Romans 4:25).

Therefore being justified by faith, we have peace with God through our Lord Jesus Christ (Romans 5:l)

For he has made him to be sin for us, who knew no sin; that we might be made the righteousness of God in him (Romans 5:21).

A Little About Abram

Although Abram had been demonstrating his faith through his actions, it was still his belief in the Lord, not just his action alone, that would have made Abram right with God (Romans 4:1-5).

We too can have a right relationship with God by trusting Him after having repented of our deeds. Acts 17:30, tells us that God winked at the ignorance of man but now commanded that man everywhere must repent.

A right relationship is passed on faith the (heartfelt) inner confidence that God is who He say He is and does what He says He will do. Right actions will follow naturally as by products such as Abram after repentance. Keep in mind, your feelings have nothing to do with your spiritual walk with God through our Lord Jesus Christ. You must do this by faith and your belief in God only, even in repenting. If you don't believe by faith that God will do that He says He will do, there is no need of worshiping Him.

In Whom We Have Forgiveness (Colossians 1:9-14)

Having Forgiveness of Sins: Sometimes we wonder how to pray for those who mistreat you, not only them, but for missionaries and other leaders as well.

The Bible teaches us how and what we can faithfully pray for other as well as for missionaries and leaders we have never met and those have wronged us, these are the five different chapters we can read and learn from.

1.   understand God's will

2. gain spiritual wisdom
3. please and honor God
4. bear good fruit
5. grow in the knowledge of God
6. be filled with God's strength
7. have great endurance and patience, and eight
8. stay full of Christ's joy
9. give thanks always

Five Different Ways to Pray with References

All believers have these basic needs. God has given to all believers through Christ. Read these five chapters.

1. He made us qualified to share His inheritance (2-Corinthians 5:21)
2. He rescued us from Satan's dominion of darkness and made us His children (Colossians 2:15)
3. He brought us into His eternal kingdom (Ephesians 1 :5-6)
4. He redeemed us bought our freedom from sin and judgment (Hebrews 9:12)
5. He forgave all our sins (Ephesians 1:7)

Thank God for what you have received in Christ Jesus our Lord

We are Complete in Christ Jesus

For in him dwelled all the fullness of the Godhead bodily. And you are complete in him, which is the head of all Principality and power: In whom also you are circumcised with the circumcision made without hands, in putting of the body of the sins of the flesh by the circumcision of Christ: Buried with him in baptism, wherein also you are raised with him through the faith of the operation of God, and you, being dead in your sins and the uncircumcision of your flesh, has he quicken together with him, having forgiven you all trespasses; blotting out the handwriting of ordinance that was against us, which was contrary to us, and took it out of the way, nailing it to his cross (Colossians 2:9-14).

REDEMPTION THROUGH CHRIST (Isaiah 43:1)

<u>We Have Been Redeemed</u>: Life begins with God and ends with him. God's sorrow over the spiritual decay of his people. This we read in (Isaiah 43:1), God says that despite the people's spiritual failure, he will show them mercy, bring them back from captivity, and restore them.

He would give them an outpouring of love, not wrath. Then the world would know that God alone had done this. This is the love God showed to Oh, Jacob also to Oh, Israel in asking to fear not: they are the redeemed of God; he also called them by their name.

If one would go in their own strength, you are more likely to drown. If you would invite the Lord to go with you he will protect you; not only inviting him, but if you would only except him as the Lord of your life and keep him commandment, he will do things in a way that you don't have to ask, he will protect you just as he has said to Jacob, and Israel, he showed love to them, so what make you think he will do more for them than what he will do for you, do you think he love them more then you?

God asked Jacob, and Israel to fear not. He said I have redeemed you, he has called them by their name; he said also you are mine. When you go through waters, he would be with them, and through the rivers, they shall not overflow them; when they walk through the fire, they shall not be burned; neither shall the flame kindle upon them; he said he is the Lord their God, the Holy One of Israel, your Savior (Isaiah 43:1-3).

God Had Visited and Redeemed His People

Zechariah prophesied the coming of a Savior who would redeem his people and he predicted that his son John would prepare the Messiah's way. All the Old Testament prophecies were coming true no wonder Zechariah praised God! The Messiah would come in Zechariah's lifetime, and his son had been chosen to pave the way.

Blessed be the Lord God of Israel; for he has visited and redeemed his people, and has risen up a horn of salvation for us in the house of his servant (Luke 1:68-69).

Saved From Our Enemies (Luke 1:68-76)

The Jews eagerly awaiting the Messiah, but they thought he would come to save them from the powerful Roman Empire. They were ready for a military Savior, but not for a peaceful Messiah who would conquer sin.

This was God's promise to (Abraham) to (bless all people through him) (Genesis 12:3). It would be fulfilled through the (Messiah), and (Abraham's descendant). Zechariah had just recalled of years of God's sovereign work in history, beginning with Abraham and going on into eternity. Although God has unlimited power, he chooses to work through frail humans who begin as helpless babies. Don't minimize what God can do through those who are faithful to him.

What We Must Do and Be Blessed:
We should be saved from our enemies, and from the hand of all that hate us;
[72] to perform the mercy promised to our fathers, and to remember his holy covenant;
[73] the oath which he swore to our (father Abraham), that he would grant unto us, that we being delivered out of the hand of our enemies might serve him without fear,
[75] In holiness and righteousness before him, all the days of our life.
[76] And your child, shall be called the prophet of the Highest: for you shall go before the face of the Lord to prepare his ways;
[77] too give knowledge of salvation unto his people by the remission of their sins,
[78] Through the tender mercy of our God; whereby the dayspring from on high had visited us,
[79] To give light to them who sit in darkness and in the shadow of death, to guide our feet into the way of peace. (Luke 1:71-79).

CHRIST A HARMONY OF THE GOSPELS

All four books in the Bible that tell the story of Jesus Christ; (Matthew), (Mark), (Luke), and (John) stand alone, emphasizing A unique aspect of Jesus' life. But when these are blended into one complete account, or harmonized, We gain new insights about the life of Christ. This harmony combines the four Gospels into a single account of Christ's Life on earth; It includes every chapter and verse of each Gospel, leaving nothing out.

The Harmony is Divided into 250 Events: The title of each event is identical to the title found in the corresponding Gospel. The title found in more than one Gospel has identical titles, helping you to identify them quickly; each of the 250 events in the harmony is numbered.

The number of the event corresponds to the numbers next to the title in the Bible text. When reading one of the Gospel accounts, you will notice, at times, that some numbers are missing or out of sequence. The easiest way to locate these events is to refer to the harmony.

In addition, if you are looking for a particular event in the life of Christ, the harmony can help you locate it more rapidly than paging through all four Gospels. Each of the 250 events has a distinctive title keyed to the main remember of the passage to help you locate and remember the events.

The harmony will help to better visualize the travels of Jesus, study the four Gospels comparatively, and appreciate the unity of their message. There are fourteen pages of these 250 events of Christ Jesus. Number One opens with the birth of Jesus Christ.

CHART #1: Birth and Preparation of Jesus Christ

		Matt.	Mark	Luke	John
1.	Luke's purpose in writing			1:1-4	
2.	God became a human being				1:1-18
3.	The ancestors of Jesus	1:1-17		3:23-38	
4.	An angel promises the birth of John			1:5-25	
5.	An angel promises the birth of Jesus			1:26-38	
6.	Mary visits Elizabeth			1:39-56	
7.	John the Baptist is Born			1:57-80	
8.	An angel appears to Joseph	1:18-25			
9.	Jesus born in Bethlehem			2:1-7	
10.	Shepherds visit Jesus			2:8-20	
11.	Mary and Joseph bring Jesus to the temple			2:21-40	
12.	Visitors from eastern lands	2:1-12			
13.	Escape to Egypt	2:13-18			
14.	Return to Nazareth	2:19-23			
15.	Jesus speaks with the religious leaders			2:41-25	
16.	John the Baptist prepares the way	3:1-12	1:1-8	3:1-18	

CHART#1: Birth and Preparation of Jesus Christ (continued)

		Matt.	Mark	Luke	John
17.	John baptizes Jesus	3:13-17	1:9-11	3:21-22	
18.	Satan tempts Jesus in the desert	4:1-11	1:12-13	4:1-13	
19.	John the Baptist declares his mission			1:19-28	
20.	John the Baptist proclaims Jesus as the Messiah		1:29-34		
21.	The first disciples follow Jesus			1:35-51	
22.	Jesus turns water into wine			2:1-12	

CHART #2: Message and Ministry of Jesus Christ

		Matt.	Mark	Luke	John
23.	Jesus clears the temple				2:12-25
24.	Nicodemus visits Jesus at night				3:1-21
25.	John the Baptist tells more about Jesus				3:22-36
26.	Herod puts John in prison			3:19-20	
27.	Jesus talks to a woman at the well				4:1-26
28.	Jesus tells about the spiritual harvest				4:27-38
29.	Many Samaritans believe in Jesus				4:39-42
30.	Jesus preaches in Galilee	4:12-17	1:14-15	4:14-15	4:43-45
31.	Jesus heals a government official's son				4:46-54
32.	Jesus rejected in Nazareth				4:16-30

CHART #3: Message and Ministry of Jesus Christ (continued)

		Matt.	Mark	Luke	John
33.	Four fishermen follow Jesus	4:18-22	1:16-28		
34.	Jesus teaches with great authority		1:21-28	4:31-37	
35.	Jesus heals Peter's mother-in-law	8:14-17	1:29-34	4:38-41	
36.	Jesus preaches throughout Galilee	4:23-25	1:35-39	4:42-44	
37.	Jesus provides miracle of fish			5:1-11	
38.	Jesus heals a man with leprosy	8:1-4	1:40-45	5:12-16	
39.	Jesus heals a paralyzed man	9:1-8	2:1-12	5:17-26	
40.	Jesus eats with sinners at Matthew's house	9:9-13	2:13-17	5:27-32	
41.	Religious leaders ask Jesus about fasting	9:14-17	2:18-22	5:33-39	
42.	Jesus heals a lame man by the pool				5:1-18
43.	Jesus claims to be God's son				5:19-30
44.	Jesus supports his claim				5:31-47
45.	The disciples pick wheat on the Sabbath	12:1-8	2:23-28	6:1-5	
46.	Jesus heals a man's hand on the Sabbath	12:9-14	3:1-6	6:6-11	

CHART #4: Message and Ministry of Jesus Christ (continued)

		Matt.	Mark	Luke	John
47.	Large crowds followed Jesus	12:15-21	3:7-12		
48.	Jesus selects the twelve disciples		3:13-19	6:12-16	
49.	Jesus gives the Beatitudes	5:1-12		6:17-26	
50.	Salt and light	5:13-16			
52.	Jesus teaches about angles	5:21-26			
53.	Jesus teaches about lust	5:27-30			
54.	Jesus teaches about divorce	5:31-32			
55.	Jesus teaches about vows	5:33-37			
56.	Jesus teaches about retaliation	5:38-42			
57.	Jesus teaches about loving enemies	5:43-48	6:27-36		
58.	Jesus teaches about giving to the needy	6:1-4			
59.	Jesus teaches about prayer	6:6-15			
60.	Jesus teaches about fasting	6:16-18			

CHART #5: Beatitudes (continued)

		Matt.	Mark	Luke	John
61.	Jesus teaches about money	6:19-24			
62.	Jesus teaches about worry	6:25-34			
63.	Jesus teaches about criticizing others	7:1-6		6:37-42	
64.	Jesus teaches about asking, seeking	7:7-12			
65.	Jesus teaches about the way to heaven	7:13-14			
66.	Jesus teaches about	7:15-20		6:43-45	
67.	Jesus teaches about houses built on rocks and sand	7:21-29		6:46-49	
68.	A Roman centurion demonstrates faith	8:5-13		7:1-10	
69.	Jesus raises a widow's son from the dead			7:11-17	
70.	Jesus eases John's doubt	11:1-19		7:18-35	
71.	Jesus promises rest for the soul	11:20-30			
72.	A sinful woman anoints Jesus' feet			7:36-50	

CHART #6: A Woman Accompanies Jesus

	Matt.	Mark	Luke	John
73. Woman accompanies Jesus and the disciples			8:1-3	
74. Religious leaders accuse Jesus of being under Satan's power	12:22-37	3:20-30		
75. Religious leaders ask Jesus for a miracle	12:38-45			
76. Jesus describes his true family	12:46-50	3:31-35	8:19-21	
77. Jesus tells the parable of the four soils	13:1-9	4:1-9	8:4-8	
78. Jesus explains the parable of the four soils	13:10-23	4:10-25	8:9-18	
79. The parable of the growing seed		4:26-29		
80. The parable of the weeds	13:24-30			
81. The parable of the mustard seed	13:31-32	4:30-34		
82. The parable of the yeast	13:33-35			
83. Jesus explains the parable of the weed	13:36-43			
84. The parable of the hidden treasure	13:44			
85. The parable of the pearl merchant	13:45-46			

CHART #7: Parables (continued)

	Matt.	Mark	Luke	John
86. The parable of the fishing net	13:47-52			
87. Jesus calms the storm	8:23-27	4:35-41	8:22-25	
88. Jesus sends the demons into a herd of pigs	8:28-34	5:1-20	8:26-39	
89. Jesus heals a bleeding woman	9:18-26	5:21-43	8:40-56	
90. Jesus heals the blind and mute	9:27-34			
91. The people of Nazareth refuse to believe	13:53-58	6:1-6		
92. Jesus urges disciples to pray for workers	9:35-38			
93. Jesus sends out the twelve disciples	10:1-16	6:7-16	9:1-6	
94. Jesus prepares the disciples for persecution	10:17-42			
95. Herod kills John the Baptist	14:1-12	6:14-29	9:7-9	
96. Jesus feeds five thousand	14:13-21	6:30-44	9:10-17	6:1-15
97. Jesus walks on water	14:22-23	6:45-52		6:16-21
98. Jesus heals all who touch him	14:34-36	6:53-56		

CHART #8: Jesus the True Bread

	Matt.	Mark	Luke	John
99. Jesus is the true bread				6:22-40
(100. The Jews disagree that Jesus is from heaven				6:53-56
101. Many disciples desert Jesus				6:60-71
102. Jesus teaches about inner purity	15:1-20	7:1-23		
103. Jesus sends a demon out of a girl	15:21-28	7:24-30		
104. The crowd marvels at Jesus' healings	15:29-31	7:31-37		
105. Jesus feeds four thousand	15:32-39	8:1-10		
106. Religious leaders ask for a sign in the sky	16:1-4	8:11-13		
107. Jesus warns against wrong teaching	16:5-12	8:14-21		
108. Jesus restores sight to a blind man		8:22-26		
111. Jesus transfigured on the mountain	17:1-13	9:2-13	9:28-36	
112. Jesus heals a demon possessed boy	17:14-21	9:14-29	9:37-43	
113. Jesus predicts his death the second time	17:22-23	9:30-32	9:44-45	

CHART #9: Peter Finds the Coin

	Matt.	Mark	Luke	John
114. Peter finds the coin in the fish's mouth	17:24-27			
115. The disciples argue	18:1-6	9:33-37		9:46-48
116. The disciples forbid another to use Jesus' name		9:38-41	9:49-50	
117. Jesus warns against temptation	18:7-9	9:42-50		
118. Jesus warns against looking down on others	18:10-14			
119. Jesus teaches how to treat a believer who sins	18:15-20			
120. Parable of the unforgiving debtor	18:21-35			
121. Jesus' brothers ridicule him				7:1-9
122. Jesus teaches about the cost of following him	8:18-22		9:51-62	
123. Jesus teaches openly at the temple				7:10-31
124. Religious leaders attempt to arrest Jesus				7:32-52
125. Jesus forgives an adulterous woman				7:53-8:11
126. Jesus is the light of the world				8:12-20
127. Jesus warns of the coming judgment				8:21-30

CHART #10: Jesus Speaks About God

	Matt.	Mark	Luke	John
128. Jesus speaks about God's children				8:21-30
129. Jesus states he is eternal				8:48-59
130. Jesus sends out seventy-two messengers			10:1-16	
131. The seventy-two messengers return			10:17-24	
132. Parable of the Good Samaritan			10:25-37	
133. Jesus visits Mary and Martha			10:38-42	
134. Jesus teaches the disciples about prayer			11:1-13	
135. Jesus answers hostile accusations			11:14-28	
136. Jesus warns against unbelief			11:29-32	
137. Jesus teaches about the light within			11:33-36	
138. Jesus criticizes the religious leaders			11:37-54	
139. Jesus speaks against hypocrisy			12:1-12	
140. Parable of the rich man			12:13-21	
141. Jesus warns about worry			12:22-34	
142. Jesus warns to prepare for his coming			12:35-48	
143. Jesus warns about coming division			12:49-53	
144. Jesus warns about the future crisis			12:54-59	

CHART #11: Jesus Calls the People

	Matt.	Mark	Luke	John
145. Jesus calls the people to repent			13:1-9	
146. Jesus heals the crippled woman			13:10-17	
147. Jesus teaches about the kingdom of God			13:18-21	
148. Jesus heals the man who was born blind				9:1-12
149. Religious leaders question the blind man				9:13-34
150. Jesus teaches about spiritual blindness				9:35-42
151. Jesus the Good Shepherd				10:1-21
152. Religious leaders hear Jesus at the temple				10:22-42
153. Jesus teaches about entering the kingdom			13:22-30	
154. Jesus grieves over Jerusalem			13:31-35	
155. Jesus heals a man with dropsy (palsy)			14:1-6	
156. Jesus teaches about seeking honor			14:7-14	
157. Parable of the great feast			14:15-24	
158. Jesus teaches about the cost of being a disciple			14:25-35	
159. Parable of the lost sheep			15:1-7	
160. Parable of the lost coin			15:8-10	
161. Parable of the lost son			15:11-32	
162. Parable of the shrewd manager			16:1-18	

CHART #12: Jesus Calls the People (continued)

	Matt.	Mark	Luke	John
163. Jesus tells about the rich man and the beggar			16:19-31	
164. Jesus tells about forgiveness and faith			17:1-10	
165. Lazarus becomes ill and dies				11:1-16
167. Jesus raises Lazarus from the dead				11:38-44
168. Religious leaders plot to kill Jesus				11:45-57
169. Jesus heals ten men with leprosy			17:11-19	
170. Jesus teaches about the coming of the kingdom of God			17:20-37	
171. Parable of the persistent widow			18:1-8	
172. Parable of two men who prayed			18:9-14	
173. Jesus teaches about marriage and divorce	19:1-12	10:1-12		
174. Jesus blesses little children	19:13-15	10:13-16		
175. Jesus speaks to the	19:16-30	10:17-13	18:18-30	
176. Parable of the workers paid equally	20:1-16			
177. Jesus predicts his	20:17-19	10:32-34	18:31-34	
178. Jesus teaches about serving others	20:20-28	10:35-45		
179. Jesus heals a blind	20:29-34	10:46-52	18:35-40	

CHART #13: Jesus Calls the People (continued)

		Matt.	Mark	Luke	John
180.	Jesus brings salvation to Zacchaeus' home			19:1-10	
181.	Parable of the king's ten servants			19:11-27	
182.	A woman anoints Jesus with perfume	26:6-13	14:3-9		12:1-11
183.	Jesus rides a donkey into Jerusalem	21:1-11	11:1-11	19:28-44	12:12-19
184.	Jesus clears the temple	21:12-17	11:12-17	19:45-48	
185.	Jesus explains why he must die				12:20-36
186.	Most people do not believe in Jesus				12:37-43
187.	Jesus summarizes his	12:44-50			
188.	Jesus says the disciples can pray for anything	21:18-22	11:20-26		
189.	Religious leaders challenge Jesus' authority	21:23-27	11:27-33	20:1-8	
190.	Parable of the two sons	21:28-32			
191.	Parable of the wicked tenants	21:33-46	12:1-12	20:9-19	
192.	Parable of the wedding feast	22:1-14			
193.	Religious leaders questions Jesus about paying taxes	22:15-22	12:13-17	20:20-26	

CHART #14: Religious Leaders

		Matt.	Mark	Luke	John
194.	Jesus questioned about the resurrection	22:23-33	12:18-27	20:27-40	
195.	Jesus questioned about the greatest commandment	22:34-40	12:28-34		
196.	Jesus questions the religious leaders	22:41-46	12:35-37	20:41-44	
197.	Jeans warns against the religious	23:1-12	12:38-40	20:45-47	
198.	Jesus condemns the religious leaders	23:13-36			
199.	Jesus grieves over Jerusalem again	23:37-39			
200.	A poor widow gives all she has		12:41-44	21:1-4	
201.	Jesus tells about the future	24:1-25	13:1-23	21:5-24	
202.	Jesus tells about His return	24:26-35	13:24-31	21:25-33	
203.	Jesus tells about remaining watchful	24:36-51	13:32-37	21:34-38	
204.	Parable of the ten bridesmaids	25:1-13			
205.	Parable of the loaned money	25:14-30			
206.	Jesus tells about	25:31-46			

Death and Resurrection of Jesus Christ: The following section contains the detailed stipulation of the highlighted specific ways in which expresses the death and resurrection of Christ according to the plot of the religious leaders to kill Jesus. The plot is that the Pharisees knew that the Messiah would be a descendant of David, but they didn't understand that He would be God Himself.

Reference to the Gathered Pharisees: *While the Pharisees were gathered together, Jesus asked them, saying,* **What think you of Christ? Whose son is he?** *They say unto him, the son of David* (Matthew 22:41-42).

CHART #15: Death and Resurrection of Jesus Christ

		Matt.	Mark	Luke	John
207.	Religious leaders plot to kill Jesus	26:1-5	14:1-2	22:1-2	
208.	Judas agrees to betray Jesus	26:14-16	14:10-11	22:3-6	
209.	Disciples prepare for the Passover	26:17-19	14:12-16	22:7-13	
210.	Jesus washes the disciples' feet				13:1-20
211.	Jesus and the disciples have the Last Supper	26:20-30	14:17-26	22:14-30	13:21-30
212.	Jesus predicts Peter's denial			22:31-38	13:31-38

CHART #15: Death and Resurrection of Jesus Christ (continued)

		Matt.	Mark	Luke	John
213.	Jesus is the way to the Father				14:1-14
214.	Jesus promises the Holy Spirit				14:15-31
215.	Jesus teaches about the vine and the branches				15:1-17
216.	Jesus warns about the world's hated				15:18-16
217.	Jesus teaches about the Holy Spirit				16:5-15
218.	Jesus teaches about using his name in prayer				16:16-33
219.	Jesus prays for himself				17:1-5
220.	Jesus prays for his disciples				17:6-19
221.	Jesus prays for future believers				17:20-26
222.	Jesus again predicts Peter's denial	26:31-35	14:27-31		
223.	Jesus agonizes in the garden	26:36-46	14:32-42	22:39-46	
224.	Jesus is betrayed and arrested	26:47-56	14:43-52	22:47-53	18:1-11
225.	Ananias questions Jesus				18:12-24
226.	Caiaphas questions Jesus	26:57-68	14:53-65		
227.	Peter denies knowing Jesus	26:69-75	14:66-72	22:54-65	18:25-27

CHART #16: The Council of Religious Leaders

		Matt.	Mark	Luke	John
228.	The council condemns Jesus	27:1-2	15:1	22:66-71	
229.	Judas kills himself	27:3-10			
230.	Jesus stands trial before Pilate	27:11-14	15:2-5	23:1-5	18:28-37
231.	Jesus stands trial before Herod			23:6-12	
232.	Pilate hands Jesus over to be crucified				19:16
233.	Roman soldiers mock Jesus	27:27-31	15:16-20		
234.	Jesus is led away to be crucified	27:32-34	15:21-24	23:26-31	19:17
235.	Jesus is placed on the cross	27:35:44	15:25-32	23:32-43	19:18-27
236.	Jesus dies on the cross	27:45-56	15:33-41	23:44-49	19:28-37
237.	Jesus is laid in the tomb	26:57-61	15:42-47	23:50-56	19:38-42
238.	Guards are stationed at the tomb	27:62-66			
239.	Jesus rises from the dead	28:1-7	16:1-8	24:1-12	20:1-9
240.	Jesus appears to Mary Magdalene		16:9-11		20:10-18

CHART #17: Jesus Appears to the Women

		Matt.	Mark	Luke	John
241.	Jesus appears to the women	28:8-10			
242.	Religious leaders bribe the guards	28:11-15			
243.	Jesus appears to two believers traveling on the road		6:12-13	24:13-35	
244.	Jesus appears to the disciples behind locked doors			24:36-43	20:19-23
245.	Jesus appears to Disciple Thomas		16:14		20:24-31
246.	Jesus appears to fishing disciples				21:1-14
247.	Jesus talks with Peter				21:15-25
248.	Jesus gives the Great Commission	28:16-20	16:15-18		
249.	Jesus appears to the disciples in Jerusalem			24:44-49	
250.	Jesus ascends into heaven		16:19-20	24:50-53	

This concludes the charts of the 250 events of the life of Christ as the harmony of the four Gospels which are Matthew, Mark, Luke and John. These four Gospels being in agreement of the actual events of the life of Jesus during his ministry, death and resurrection. The structure of the terms of the arrangement will help the studying of the structure better as well as finding the Scriptures. This way of arrangement will help you also to better visualize the travels of Jesus. Study the four Gospels unity in which they are intended. In the message is a blessing. Learn as much as you can and get it into your spirit and it will become a part of your every-day life.

THE SPIRITUAL MINISTRY OF RECONCILIATION
(2-Corinthians 5:18-19)

Reconciliation Through Christ

God brings us back to himself through reconciliation by blotting out our sin and making us righteous.

The Word says, To wit, that God was in Christ, reconciling the world unto himself, not imputing their trespasses unto them; and have committed unto us the word of reconciliation, according to (2Cornthians 5:19).

We are no longer God's enemies, or strangers or foreigners to him, we were once like the "circumcision" considered all non-Jews (the "uncircumcised") Jews were unclean they thought of themselves as pure and clean because of their national heritage and religious establishment with God, they were to be God's people.

The Bible pointed out that Jews and Gentiles alike were unclean before God and needed to be cleansed by Christ. In order to realize how great a gift of salvation is, we need to remember our former natural, unclean condition. No one is alienated from Christ's love or from the body of believers.

Jews and Gentiles alike could be guilty of spiritual pride, Jews for thinking their faith and traditions elevated them above everyone else, Gentiles for trusting in their achievements, power or position. Spiritual pride blinds us to our own faults and magnifies the faults of others. Be careful not to become proud of your salvation.

Before Christ's coming, Gentiles and the Jews kept apart from one another. Jews considered Gentiles beyond God's saving power and therefore they were without hope. Gentiles resented Jewish claims. Christ breaks down the walls of prejudice, and reconciles all who believe in the word of God, and unifies us in one body that is Jesus Christ. He is our Lord; He is the church and we are a part of that body which makes up the church of God through Jesus Christ.

The Middle Wall Partition: *[13] But now in Christ Jesus you who sometime were far off are made nigh by the blood of Christ; [14] For he is our peace, who has made both one, and has broken down the middle wall of partition between us; [15] Having abolished in his flesh the enmity, even the law of commandments contained in ordinances; for to make in himself of twain one new man, so making peace; [16] And that he might reconcile both unto God in one body by the cross, having slain the enmity thereby; [17] And came and preached peace to you which were afar off, and to them who were nigh; [18] For through him we both have access by one Spirit unto the Father* (Ephesians 2:13-18).

Chart: Our True Identity in Christ

Romans 3:24 ....We are justified (declared "not guilty of sin).

Romans 8:1 ....No condemnation awaits us.

Romans 8:2 ....We are set free from the law of sin and death.

1-Corinthians 1:30....We are righteous and holy in Christ.

l-Corinthians 15:22 ..We will be made alive at the resurrection.

2-Cornthians 5:17.....We are a new creation.

2-Cornthians 5:21.....We receive God's righteousness.

Galatians 3:28 ....We are one in Christ with all other believers.

Ephesians 1:3............We are blessed with every spiritual blessing in Christ Jesus.

Ephesians 1:4............We are holy, blameless, and covered with God's love.

Ephesians 1:5-6.........We are adopted as God's children.

Ephesians 1:7............Our sins are taken away and we are forgiven.

Ephesians 1:10-11.....We will be brought under Christ's headship

Ephesians 1: 13.........We are marked as belonging to God by the Holy Spirit.

Ephesians 2:6............We have been raised up to sit with Christ in glory.

Ephesians 2:10..........We are God's workmanship created in Christ Jesus.

Ephesians 2:13..........We have been brought near to God.

Ephesians 3:6............We share in the promise in Christ

Ephesians 3:12..........We can come with freedom and confidence into
God's body, the church.

Ephesians 5:29-30.....We are members of Christ's body, the church.

Colossians 2:10.........We have been given fullness in Christ.

Colossians.................We are set free from our sinful nature.

2-Timonthy 2:10.......We will have eternal glory.

IN THE REGENERATION (Matthew 19:28)

Regeneration

Regeneration is the spiritual change brought about in a person's life by and act of God. In regeneration a person's sinful nature is changed, and he is enabling to respond to God by faith. The word regeneration occurs only in the New Testament in saying he saved us, by the washing of regeneration in (Titus 3:5). Matthew says, *you which have followed me, in the regeneration when the Son of man shall sit in the throne of his glory, you also shall sit upon twelve thrones, judging the twelve tribes of Israel* (Matthew 19:28).

The concept or idea is common throughout the Bible. The literal meaning of regeneration is "born again." The need for regeneration grows out of humanity's sinfulness. It is brought about through God's work in the human heart, and the person responds to God through faith.

Regeneration is an act of God through the Holy Spirit, which resulting in resurrection from sin to a new life in Jesus Christ (2-Corinthians 5:17). Christians are brand new people in Christ Jesus.

The Holy Spirit gives them a new life, and they are not the same anymore. We are not reformed, rehabilitated, or reeducated we are recreated (a new creation), living in union with Christ Jesus. At conversion we are not merely turning over a new leaf, we are beginning a new life under a new Master.

Therefore if any man be in Christ, he is a new creature: old things are passed way; behold all things are become new (2-Corinthians 5:17).

Receiving Christ as Lord of your life is the beginning of life with Christ. As you have therefore received Christ Jesus the Lord, so walk you in him: rooted and build up in him, and established in the faith, as you have been taught, abounding therein with thanksgiving (Colossians 2:6-7).

The Beginning of Life with Christ

Receiving Christ as Lord of your life is the beginning of life with Christ. You must continue to follow his leadership by being rooted, built up, and strengthened in the faith.

Christ wants to guide you and help you with your daily problems. You can live for Christ by

1.   committing your life to him and submitting your will to him (Romans 12:1-

2).2.   seeking to learn from him, his life, and his teachings (Colossians 3:16).and
3.   recognizing the Holy Spirit's power in you (Acts 1:8).(Galatians 5:22).

<u>Illustration of Being Rooted in Christ</u>: As a illustration of being rooted in Christ, would be that of plants that draw nourishment from the soil through their roots, so we draw our life giving strength from Christ. The more we draw our strength from Him, the less we will be fooled by those who falsely claim to have life's answers. If Christ is our strength, we will be free from human regulations. If we read nothing more, we can't help but to grow in grace and be blessed of God through Christ Jesus.

GRACE AND MERCY

Grace: Grace shoes favor or kindness without regard to the worthiness or merit of the one who receives it and in spite of what that person deserves he receive grace. God is "merciful and gracious, long-suffering, and abounding in goodness and truth." Therefore, grace is almost always associated with mercy, love and patience as the source of help and deliverance from distress. (Exodus34:6; Exodus 20:16).(Jeremiah 31:28-30).

- God Makes a New Covenant with the House of Israel: Jeremiah 31:31.

- The Meanings of the Proverb Concerning the Sour: Ezekiel 18:2-13, 17-32.

The Covenant Was not made with the Fathers: Now according to the covenant God made with the fathers, He made a new Covenant with the house of Israel and with Judah (Ezekiel 18:32).(Jeremiah 31:32).

But this shall be the covenant that I will make with the house of Israel; after those days, said the Lord, I will put my law in their inward parts, and write it in their hearts; and will be their God, and they shall be my people (Hebrews 8:8-13; 9:1-2; 11-12).

Now Jeremiah's teaching is that the children shall not be teaching any more. This proves because God will put His law into the hearts of the people and they will be His people and He will be their God (Jeremiah 31:33).

God Shows Loving Kindness: (Jeremiah 32:18-19).(Ezekiel 18:3-6). Read Ezekiel 18:3-31 to more fully understand that we received Adam's sin because he brought sin into the world. Yes sin is in the world because of Adam, but we don't have to sin because of it. God has given us the power over sin, even the temptations we are faced with He gives us a way out. Scripture concerning temptation: (Galatians 4:14).(James 1:2-5).1-John 5:4; 14-15).1-Timothy 6:9).1-Peter 2:9-10).1-Corinthians 10:13).

Cowardly Running Away

Running away is sometimes considered cowardly, but a wise person realizes that removing themselves physically from temptation often can be the most courageous action to take. Here again the Bible teaches us that a young man was warned to flee anything that produced evil thoughts.

Do you have a recurring temptation that is difficult to resist? If so, remove yourself physically from any condition that will stimulate your desire to sin. Knowing when to flee is as important in spiritual battle as knowing when and how to fight.

Flee also youthful lust: but follow righteousness, faith, charity, with them who call on the Lord out of a pure heart (2- Timothy 2:22).

<u>The Bible Uses Actions</u>: The Bible uses active and forceful verbs to describe the Christian life: Pursue, fight, and take hold. Some think Christianity is a passive religion that advocates waiting for God to act. But we must have an active faith, obeying God with courage and doing what we know is right. Is it time for action on your part?

You Oh man of God, flee these things; and follow after righteousness, godliness, faith, love, patience, meekness; fight the good fight of faith, lay hold on eternal life, whereunto you are also called, and has professed a good profession before many witnesses 1-Timothy 6:12-13).

IN TIME OF TEMPTATION (Luke 8:13)

People on the Rock: "Path" people, like many of the religious leaders, refused to believe God's message. "Rock" people, like many in the crowds who follow Jesus, believed His message but never got around to doing anything about it. "Thorn path" people, overcome by worries and the lure of doctrine that everything in the world, including thoughts, will, and feelings can be explained only in terms of matter; the tendency to be more concern with material then with spiritual values. These are people who left no room in their lives for God "Good soil" people, in contrast to all the other groups, followed Jesus no matter what the cost. Which type of soil are you in?

They on the rock are they, which, when they hear, receive the word with joy, and these have no root, which for a while believe, and in time of temptation fall away (Luke 8:13).

Illness and Pain: Paul had a sickness that was causing him to have pain in his body, yet he endured it while he was visiting the Galatians church. The world is often callous to people's pain and misery. Even though Paul's condition was a trial to him he didn't explain what was wrong with him.

Such caring was what Jesus meant when He called us to serve the homeless, hungry, sick, and imprisoned as if they were Jesus himself (Matthew 25:34-40). Do you avoid those in pain or those facing difficulty or are you willing to care for them as if they were Jesus Christ Himself?

Hurtful Lusts: I would like to use this statement to show the spiritual aspect of growth in a Christian's walk with the Lord. This is the key to spiritual growth and personal fulfillment. We would honor God and center our desires on him through godliness according to Matthew, and we should be content with what God is doing in our lives.

Temptations Leading to Spiritual Weakness (1-Timothy 6:9)
These following three references should help in understanding lust after money and lusts after things of this world. These are temptations that lead to spiritual weakness.

But they that will be rich fall into temptation and a snare, and into many foolish and hurtful lusts, which drown men in destruction and perdition (1-Timothy 6:9).

But seek first the kingdom of God and his righteousness and all these things will be given to you as well (Matthew 6:33).

Not that I speak in respect of want: for I have learned, in Whatsoever state I am, therewith to be content. I know both how to be abased, and I know how to abound: Everywhere and in all things I am instructed both to be full and to be hungry, both to abound and to suffer need. I can do all things through Christ which strengthened me (Philippians 4:11-13).

Five References: How to Distinguish Your Needs

Despite of the overwhelming evidence to the contrary of spiritual life, people still believe that money brings happiness. Rich people craving greater riches can be caught in an endless cycle that only ends in ruin and destruction. This leads to a big question: How can you keep away from the love of money? The Bible gives us some guidelines:

1.   <u>Realizing that one day all riches will all be gone</u> for we brought nothing into this world, and it is certain we can carry nothing out. *Charge them who are rich in this world, that they be not high-minded nor trust in uncertain riches, but in the living God, who gives us richly all things to enjoy 1-Timothy 6:7, 17).*

2.   <u>Be content with what you have</u>. *And having food and raiment let us be therewith content 1-Timothy 6:8)*

3.   <u>Monitor what you are willing to do to get more money</u>. *But they that will be rich fall into temptation and a snare, and into many and hurtful lusts, which drown men in destruction and perdition; For the love of money is the root of all evil: which while some coveted after, they have erred from the faith, and pierced themselves through with many sorrows 1-Timothy 6:9-10).*

4.   <u>Love people more than money</u>. *But you, Oh man of God, flee these things; and follow after righteousness, godliness faith, love patience, meekness 1-Timothy 6: 11).*

5.   <u>Love God's work more than money</u>. 1-Timothy 6:11 is the same in loving, the difference is one is saying love man more than money the other is loving God more than money. *Love God's work more than money (l-Timothy 6:11).*

6.   <u>Freely share what you have with others</u>. *That they do good that they be rich in good works, ready to distribute, willing to communicate 1-Timothy 6:18).*

Read Proverbs to learn more about avoiding the love of money .

Ethical Teachings From a Biblical Point of View

Two things have I required of you; deny me not before I die. Remove far from me vanity and lies: give me neither the condition or quality of being poor; nor riches; feed me with food convenient for me. Lest I be full, and deny you, and say, who is the Lord? Or lest I be poor, and steal, and take the name of my God in vain (Proverbs 30:7-9).

So again, it is helpful to distinguish between needs and wants. We may have all we need to live but let ourselves become discontented over what we merely want. We can choose to be content without having all that we want. The only alternative is to be a slave to our desire.

The biblical teachings are that greed leads to all kinds of evil. This is a very good illustration: problems in marriage are something that will cause evil thinking and deeds; it can lead to robbery or a blowup in partnership. To master greed you must control it at its root. Get rid of the desire to be rich and to have that you can't, and be content in the works of God through Christ Jesus 1-Timnthy 6:10)

Glory in Tribulation

In biblical thinking and ethical speaking, whenever we face trials it is very possible to profit from them. You will understand this more as we go on with the understanding of temptation. The point is not to pretend to be happy when we face pain, but to have a positive outlook ("consider it pure joy") because of what trials can produce in our lives.

The Bible teaches us to turn our hardships into a time of learning. Times in being tough biblically speaking, it can teach us perseverance. Search for other passages dealing with perseverance (also called patience and steadfastness).

1.   Counting all Things Joy. *To them who by patient continuance in well doing seek for glory and honor and mortality, eternal life* (Romans 2:7).

2.   Glory in Tribulation. *And not only so, but we glory in tribulation also knowing that tribulation work patience; and patience, experience; and experience, hope: and hope make not ashamed; because the love of God is shed abroad in our hearts by the Holy Ghost which is given unto us* (Romans 5:3-5).

3.   We are Saved by Hope. *For we are saved by hope: but hope that is seen is not hope: for what a man see, why do he yet hope for? But if we hope for that we see not, and then do we with patience wait for it* (Romans 8:24-25)

4.   Giving no Offence in Anything. *Giving no offence in any-thing, that the ministry be not blamed: But in all things approving ourselves as the ministers of God, in much patience, in affliction, in necessities, in distresses, in stripes, in imprisonments, in tumults, in labors, in watching, in fasting; By pureness, by knowledge, by longsuffering, by kindness, by the Holy Ghost, by love unfeigned, by the word of truth, by the power of God, by the amour of righteousness on the right hand and on the left* (2-Corinthians 6:3-7).

5.   Grace and Peace be Multiplied Unto You. *Grace and peace be multiplied unto you through the knowledge of God, and of Jesus our Lord, according as his divine power has given unto us all things that pertain unto life and godliness, through the knowledge of him that has called us to glory and virtue. Whereby are given unto us exceeding great and precious promises; that by these might be partakers of the divine nature, having escaped the corruption*

that is in the world through lust. And beside this giving all diligence, add to your faith virtue; and to virtue knowledge; and to knowledge temperance; and to temperance patience; and to patience godliness; and to godliness brotherly kindness; and to brotherly kindness charity. For if these things be in you, and abound, they make you that you shall neither be barren nor unfruitful in the knowledge of our Lord Jesus Christ. But he who lack these things is blind, and cannot see afar off, and have forgotten that he was purged from his old sins (2-Peter 1:2-9).

God Knows How to Deliver

Just as God rescued Lot from Sodom, remember He can and is able to rescue us from the temptation and trials we face in a wicked world. He also will give us the chance to rescue ourselves through His word.

In asking to awake that sleep, and arise from the dead, and Christ shall give you light (Ephesians 5:14).

God is no different today than He was yesterday. Look at Lot; he was not sinless, but he put his trust in God and was spared when Sodom was destroyed. God also will judge those who cause temptations and trials, so we need never worry about justice being done.

And delivered just Lot, vexed with the filthy conversation of the wicked; for that righteous man dwelling among them, in seeing and hearing, vexed his righteous soul from day to day with their unlawful deeds; the Lord, knows how to deliver the godly out of temptation, and to reserve the unjust unto the Day of Judgment to be punished (2-Peter 2:7-9).

Some people simply drift through life. Their choices are as such, when they can muster the will to choose, they tend to follow the course of least resistance. Aren't we all are somewhat alike in that life giving way of being? God has given us a way out but we don't seem to care enough to take the chance of accepting the gift of faith in a way of *trusting in the Lord with all our hearts, and leaning not unto our own understanding; but in all our ways acknowledging him, letting him direct our paths* (Proverbs 3:5-6)

A Brief Profile of Lot

<u>During Lot's Youth</u>: When Lot lost his father it must have been hard on him. He was not left without strong role models in his life which were his grandfather (Torah) and his (Uncle Abram), who raised him.

Still, Lot did not develop their sense of purpose. Throughout his life he was so caught up in the present moment that he seemed incapable of seeing the consequences of his actions. It is hard to imagine what his life would have been like without (Abram's

41

careful attention and God's intervention.

By the time Lot drifted out of the picture, his life had taken an ugly turn. He had blended into the sinful culture of his day that he did not want to leave it. His drifting finally took him in a very specific direction of destruction.

Lot is called "righteous" in the New Testament. Let us read what it says concerning Lot in 2-Peter 2:7-8. *And delivered just Lot, vexed with the filthy conversation of the wicked,* we read previously about Lot being vexed with the filthy conversation of the wicked. Here we are seeing it differently where, before we just saw how he delivered. Now we are looking at him being a righteous man dwelling among them, *in seeing and hearing, vexed his righteous soul from day to day with their unlawful deeds* (2-Peter 2:7-8).

Ruth, a descendant of Moab, was an ancestor of Jesus, even though Moab was born as a result of Lot's incestuous relationship with one of his daughters. Lot's story gives hope to us that God forgives and often brings about positive circumstances from evil.

A Question for You. What is the direction of your life? Are you headed toward God or away from him? If you're a drifter, the choice for God may seem difficult, but it is the one choice that puts all other choices in a different light.

Lot's Strengths and Accomplishments

1.   Strengths and Accomplishments. He was a successful businessman. Peter calls him a righteous man (2-Peter 2:7-8)

2.   Weakness and Mistakes. When faced with decisions, he tended to put off deciding, then chose the easiest course of action. When given a choice, his first reaction was to think of himself.

3.   Lesson From Lot's Life. God wants us to do more than drift through life; He wants us to be an influence for Him. The lesson showed how God can deliver His people.

4.   Vital Statistics. Lot first lived first in Dr of the Chileans, then moved to Canaan with Abram. Eventually he moved to the wicked city of Sodom Lot was a wealthy sheep and cattle rancher and also a city official. Lot's father was Haran Adopted by Abram when his father died. The name of his wife, who turned into a pillar of salt, is not mentioned.

5.   Key Verse. When he hesitated, the men grasped his hand and the hands of his wife and of his two daughters and led them safely out of the city, for the Lord was merciful to them. *And while he lingered, the men laid hold upon his hand, and upon the hand*

of his wife, and upon the hand of his two daughters; the Lord being merciful unto him: and they brought him forth, and set him without the city (Genesis 19:16).

Lot's story is told in (Genesis 19:11-14). He is also mentioned in Deuteronomy 2:9, Luke 17:28-32, and 2-Peter 2:7-8).

Strong Encouragement (1-Corinthians 10:13)

The Bible gives strong encouragement to Christian today concerning temptation. Wrong desire and temptation happen to everyone; don't feel that you are singled out. Others have resisted temptation and you can also. Any temptation can be resisted because God will help in resisting it, if you turn to Him.

Once you recognize those people and situations that give you trouble, turn from it or them. Choose to do only what is right, pray for God's help, and seek friends who love God enough to that which is right before God's eyes.

The Bible teaches there has no temptation taken you but such as is common to man, but God is faithful, who will not suffer you to be tempted above that you are able; but will with the temptation also make a way to escape, that you may be able to bear it, this saying is according to 1-Corinthians 10:13)

<u>More Words of Encouragement</u>: Some believe that *I will also keep you from hour of trial* means there will be a future time of great tribulation from which true believers will be spared. The church will go through the time of tribulation and that God will keep them strong in the midst of it. Still others believe this refers to time of great distress in general, the church's suffering through the ages. Whatever the case, our emphasis should be on obeying God no matter what we may face. The Bible gives very good reasons why we should rely on God's word.

Because you have kept the word of my patience, I also will keep you from the hour of temptation, which shall come upon all the world, to try them who dwell upon the earth (Revelation 3:10).

<u>Obedience and Fidelity</u>: Obedience, fidelity, and free confession of the name of Christ, are the fruits of true grace, and are pleasing to Christ as such. Here is a promise of the great favor God would bestow on this church. This favor consists in two things: Christ would make this church's enemies subject to her

Behold, I will cause those of the synagogue of Satan, who say they are Jews, and are not, but lie behold, I will make them to come and bow down at your feet, and to know that I have loved you; Because you have kept the Word of my perseverance, I also will keep you from hour of testing, that hour which is about to come upon the whole world, to test those who dwell upon the earth (Revelation 3:9-10).

The Door of Liberty: These were proper characters for Him, when speaking to a church that had endeavored to be conformed to Christ in holiness and truth, and that had enjoyed a wide door of liberty and opportunity under His care and government. The subject matter of this epistle where Christ puts them in mind of what He had done for them: *Jesus said,* ***I have set before you an open door, and no man can shut it, I have set it open, and kept it open, though there be many adversaries.***

I know your work: behold, I have set before you an open door, and no man can shut it: for you have a little strength, and have kept my word, and have not denied my name (Revelation 3:8)

You have a little strength, a little grace, which it be not proportionate to the wide door of opportunity which I have opened to you, yet is true grace, and has kept you faithful. True grace, though it is weak, it has the divine approbation; although Christ accepts a little strength, yet believers should not rest being satisfied in a little, but should strive to grow in grace, to be strong in faith, giving glory to God. True grace, although it is weak, will do more than the greatest gifts or highest degrees of common grace, for it will enable the Christian to keep the word of Christ, and not to deny his name. We have talked about this before.

In Times of Great Stress: In times of stress we are vulnerable to temptation even if we have a willing spirit. Jesus gave us an example of what to do to resist. There are three biblical teachings for those who believe in God.

Pray
And he went forward a little, and fell on the ground and prayed that, if it were possible, the hour might pass from him (Mark 14:35).

Seek Support of Friends and Loved Ones: *And he took with him Peter and James and John and began to be sore afraid and to be very heavy hearted; and he came and found them sleeping and said unto Peter, Simon, sleep you? Couldn't not you watch one hour? And when he returned he found them asleep again for their eyes were heavy, neither wits they what to answer him, and he come the third time, and said unto them, sleep on now, and take your rest: It is enough, the hour is come; behold, the Son of man is betrayed Into the hands of sinners* (Mark 14:33,37, 40-41).

Focus on the Purpose God has Given Us: *And he said, Ababa, Father, all things are possible unto you; take this cup from me: nevertheless not what I will, but what your will* (Mark 14:36).

Watch and Pray: *Watch and pray, lest you enter into temptation. The spirit truly is ready, but the flesh is weak* (Mark 14:38).

Attitude of Trust and Confidence

The Boy Possessed by a Spirit: This is a story concerning a man having a young son having a dumb spirit which tears him. The father went to the disciples in hopes that they would cast out the spirit but they could not. *Jesus said,* ***Oh faithless generation, how long shall I be with you? How long shall I suffer you? Bring him unto me.***

The Scripture says that the father brought the son to Jesus: and when He saw the boy straightway the spirit tore at him; and he fell on the ground, and wallowed foaming. Jesus asked the father, how long is it since this came unto him? The father said from a child.

The disciples didn't have faith enough to cast out the spirit, just like some of us today who are following Jesus don't have faith enough to go through life without being able to resist temptation, yet they say they are full of the Holy Spirit

Faith of the Boy's Father: Read (Mark 9:14-29). The father said to Jesus concerning the boy that oftentimes the boy has been cast into the fire, and into the water, to destroy him: but if you can do anything, have compassion on us, and help us. Jesus said unto the father, ***If you can believe, all things are possible to him that believe.*** The father of the child cried out, and said with tears, Lord, I believe; help my unbelief.

Having the attitude of trust and confidence is not something we can obtain without help, Just as the father needed the help of Jesus to ask him or say to him, all things are possible if he believe, that is when the father cried with tears saying Lord I believe.

Faith is a gift from God, no matter how much faith we have, we never reach the point of being self-sufficient, just as the father was not sufficient enough to cast out the spirit out of his son. You can't substitute faith any more than prayer. It isn't something that you can store away like money. It is done through the works of God through Jesus Christ. God will do or be in some way to show that you can have faith in Him as well as His Son. Growing in faith is a constant process of daily renewing our trust in God through Christ Jesus.

Vital Statistics:
1.   Purpose. To present the person, work and teachings of Jesus.

2.   Author. John Mark was not one of the twelve disciples but he accompanied Paul on his first missionary journey (Acts 13:13).

3.   To Whom Written. The Christians in Rome where he wrote the Gospels.

4.   Date Written. Between A.D. 55 and 65.

5.   Setting. The Roman Empire under Tiberius Caesar. The empire with its common language and excellent transportation and communication systems was ripe to hear Jesus' message, which spread quickly from nation to nation.

6.   Key People. Jesus, the 12 disciples, Pilate, the Jewish religious leaders

7.   Key Places. Capernaum, Caesarea Philippi, Jericho, Bethany, Mount of Olives, Jerusalem, Golgotha

8.   Key Verse: *For even the Son of Man did not come to be saved, but to save and to give his life as a ransom for many* (Mark 10:45).

9.   Special Features. Mark was the first Gospel written. The other Gospels quote all but 31 verses of Mark. Mark records more miracles than any other Gospel.

10.   Overview. We're number one! The greatest, strongest, prettiest champions! Daily those proclamations assert claims of supremacy. Everyone wants to be or be with a winner. In direct contrast are the words of Jesus, ***And whoever wants to be first must be slave of all. Even the Son of Man did not come to be served, but to serve*** (Mark 10:44-45).

Enticement to Sin

An enticement or invitation to sin, with the implied promise of greater good to be derived from following the way of disobedience. In this sense God does not tempt man, nor can he himself as the holy God be tempted according to the biblical standards.

People who live for God often wonder why they still have temptation. Here is a question to you, Does God tempt people? Under a new and better covenant, therefore God does not test people by trying to seduce them into being obedience to His word. What God will do is allow Satan to tempt people, in order to refine their faith and to help them grow in their dependence on Christ's teachings. We can resist the temptation to sin by turning to God for strength and choosing to obey His Word.

Let no man say when he is tempted, I am tempted of God, for God cannot be tempted with evil, neither tempt he any man. But every man is tempted, when he is drawn away of his own lust and enticed (James 1:13-14).

Jesus is Faithful: He will stay by our side even when we have endured so much that we seem to have no faith left. We may be faithless at times but Jesus is still faithful to His promise to be with us "to the very end of the age." Refusing Christ's help will break our communication with God, but He will never turn His back on us even though we may turn our backs on Him.

If we believe not, yet he abides faithful. He cannot deny himself 1-Timothy 2:13).

Teaching them to observe all things whatsoever I have commanded you: and, Lo, I am with you always, even unto the end of the world AMEN (Matthew 28:20).

A New and Better Covenant

<u>If Our Hearts are not Changed</u>: If our hearts are not changed following God' rules will be unpleasing and difficult. We will rebel against being told how to live. The Holy Spirit gives us the new desires, helping us to want to obey God. With a new heart, we find that serving God is our greatest joy.

<u>Working out our Own Salvation</u>: *Wherefore, my beloved, as you have always obeyed, not as in my presence only, but now much more in my absence, work out your own salvation with fear and trembling. For it is God which work in you both to will and to do of his good pleasure* (Philippians 2:12-13).

<u>Under God's New Covenant</u>: God's law is inside us. It is no longer an external set of rules and principles. The Holy Spirit reminds us of Christ's words, activates our consciences, which influences our motives and desires, and makes us want to obey. Now doing God's will is something we desire will all our heart and mind.

For this is the covenant that I will make with the house of Israel after those days, said the Lord. I will put my law into their minds, and write them in their hearts; and I will be to them a God and they shall be to me a people; And they shall not teach every man his neighbor, and every man his brother, saying, know the Lord. For all shall know me, from the least to the greatest (Hebrews 8:10-11).

<u>The Supreme Tempter is Satan</u>: The supreme tempter is Satan who is able to not only play on the weakness of the corrupted human nature, but upon the children of the house hold of God as well. Jesus was able to resist all of the devil's temptations because He not only knew the Scripture He also obeyed it.

<u>Take on the Helmet of Salvation</u>: *Take the helmet of salvation, and the sword of the Spirit, which is the word of God: Praying always with all prayer and supplication in the Spirit, and watching thereunto with all perseverance and supplication for all saints* (Ephesians 6:17-18).

God's Word is a Sword

Bible verses are important. God's word is a sword to use in spiritual combat.

Knowing Bible verses is an important step in helping to resist the devil's attacks, but we must also obey the Bible ethical teachings. We must make note that Satan had memorized the Scripture, but he failed to obey it, knowing and obeying the Bible helps us to follow God's desires rather than the devil's.

Satan Knew the Scriptures: *And when the tempter came to him, he said, If you be the Son of God command that these stones be made into bread* (Matthew 4:3).

Sexual Temptation: Sexual temptations are difficult to withstand because they appeal to the normal and natural desires that God has given us. Marriage provides God's way to satisfy those natural sexual desires and to strengthen the partners against temptation. Married couples have the responsibility to care for each other. Husbands and wives should not withhold themselves sexually from one another, but should fulfill each other's needs and desires.

There has no temptation taken you but such as is common to man. But God is faithful, who will suffer you to be tempted above that you are able: but will with the temptation also make away to escape, that you may be able to bear it 1-Corinthians 10:13).

Defraud you not one the other, except it be with consent for a time, that you may give yourselves to fasting and prayer; and come together again, that Satan tempt you not for your incontinency 1-Corinthians 7:5).

The Corinthian church was in turmoil because of the immorality of the culture around them. Some Greeks, in rejecting immorality, rejected sex and marriage altogether.

Spiritually We Belong to God

Our bodies belong to God. This is the reason we belong to God, when we became Christians and because Christ bought us by paying the price to release us from sin.

What? Know you not that your body is the temple of the Holy Ghost which is in you, which you have of God, and you are not your own? For you are bought with a price. Therefore glorify God in your body, and in your spirit, which are God's (1-Corinthians 6:19-20).

God Designed Marriage for Us: Physically, our bodies belong to our spouses. Because God designed marriage so that, through the union of husband and wife, the two become one. The Bible stressed complete equality in sexual relationship. Neither male nor female should seek dominance or autonomy.

Therefore shall a man leave his father and his mother? And shall cleave unto his wife; and they shall be one flesh (Genesis 2:24).

The wife has not power of her own body, but the husband; and likewise also the husband has not power of his own body, but the wife 1-Corinthians 7:4).

Sexual pressure is not the best motive for getting married, but it is better to marry the right person than to "burn with passion." Many new believers in Corinth thought all sex was wrong, so some engaged couples were deciding to not get married.

In the Bible it is written telling couples who wanted to marry that they should not frustrate their normal sexual drives by avoiding marriage. This does not mean that people who have trouble controlling themselves should marry the first person who comes along or because of a mistake in getting with a child. It is better to deal with the pressure of desire than to deal with an unhappy marriage. AMEN. When that desire comes over you take a walk through the park.

Satan "The Tempter"

A Powerful Evil Spirit: Satan the most powerful evil spirit, can affect both the spiritual world and the physical world. Satan tempted Jesus, but Jesus was more powerful than Satan. Jesus defeated Satan when Jesus died on the cross for our sins and rose again to bring us new life. At the proper time God will overthrow Satan forever.

And you has he quickened, who were dead in trespasses and sin; Wherein in time past you walked according to the course of this world, according to the prince of the power of the air, the spirit that now works in the children of disobedience: Among whom also you all had our conversation in time past in the lusts of our flesh, fulfilling the desires of the flesh and of the mind; And were by nature the children of wrath, even as others (Ephesians 2:1-3).

Finally, my brethren, be strong in the Lord, and in the power of his might. Put on the whole amour of God, that you may be able to stand against the wiles of the evil. For we wrestle not against flesh and blood, but against principalities, against the rulers of the darkness of this world, against spiritual wickless in high places (Ephesians 6:10-12).

And lest I should be exalted above measure through the abundance of the revelation, there was given to me a thorn in the flesh, the messenger of Satan to buffet me, lest I should be exalted above measure. For this thing I besought the Lord thrice that it might depart from me. And he said unto me, my grace is sufficient for you for my strength is made perfect in weakness. Most gladly therefore will I rather glory in my infirmities, that the power of Christ may rest upon me. Therefore I take pleasure in infirmities in reproaches, in necessities, in persecution, in distresses for Christ's sake: for when I am weak, then am I strong (2- Corinthians 12:7-10).

[1] Then was Jesus led up of the Spirit into the wilderness to be tempted of the devil. [2] And when he had fasted forty days and forty nights, he was afterward hungry. [3] And when

the tempter came to him, he said, If you be the Son of God, command that these stones be made bread, [4] But he answered and said, **it is written, Man shall not live by bread a lone, but by every word that proceeds out of the mouth of God.** [5] Then the devil took him up into the holy city, and sat him on a pinnacle of the temple, [6] And said unto him, If you be the Son of God, cast yourself down, for it is written, He shall give his angels charge concerning you, and in their hands they shall bear you up, lest at any time you dash your foot against a stone. [7] Jesus said unto him, **It is written again, You shall not tempt the Lord your God.** [8] Again, the devil took him up into an exceeding high mountain and showed him all The kingdoms of the world, and the glory of them; [9] And said unto him, All these things will I give you, if you will fall down and worship me. [10] Then said Jesus unto him, **Get thee hence, Satan: for it is written, you shall worship the Lord your God, and him only shall you serve.** [11] Then the devil left him, and behold, angels came and ministered unto him. (Matthew 4:1-11).

And when the thousand years are expired Satan shall be loosed out of his prison, and shall go out to deceive the nations which are in the four quarters of the earth, Gog and Magog. To gather then together to battle the number of whom is as the sand of the sea. And they went up on the breadth of the earth, and compassed the camp of the saints about, and the beloved city: and fire came down from God out of heaven, and devoured them. And the devil that deceived them was cast into the lake of fire and brimstone, where the beast and the false prophet are, and shall be tormented day and night forever and ever (Revelation 20:7-10).

Worksheets follow. The answers will be true or false, you must answer according to the Scripture, most of all try and have a spiritual mind in answering them, otherwise, you will miss out and your answers will be wrong.

Worksheet: Temptation of Jesus

These are YES/NO questions and TRUE/FALSE taken from the K.J.V. Bible in Matthew 4:1-11.

1.	Jesus was hungry and ate before he was tempted by Satan.	True/False
2.	After Jesus had eaten he became strong.	True/False
3.	Did Jesus eat before he was tempted	True/False
4.	Was Jesus weak after he had fasted	True/False
5.	Did Jesus fast 40 or 30 nights?	True/False
6.	How long did Jesus fast? Was it 40 days and 40 nights?	YES/NO
7.	Did Jesus use his divine power to satisfy himself?	YES/NO
8.	What was Jesus' natural desire for food? Was it bread of life?	True/False
9.	Food hunger and eating are good, but the timing was wrong	True/False
10.	Why was Jesus in the desert? Was it to be tempted or to fast?	Fast/Tempt
11.	Dose fasting mean to eat when you want something to eat?	True/False
12.	Fasting makes you spiritually strong.	True/False
13.	Jesus used his divine power to change the stones to bread.	True/False
14.	Jesus was in the desert to fast.	True/False
15.		True/False
16.	Jesus gave up the unlimited, independent use of his divine power in order to experience humanity fully.	True/False
17.	We also may be tempted as Jesus was.	True/False
18.	we may be tempted to satisfy a perfectly normal desire in a wrong way or at the wrong time.	True/False
19.	If we indulge in sex before marriage or if we steal to get food, we are trying to satisfy God-given desires in wrong ways.	YES/NO
20.	God wants us to satisfy our needs and desires in the right way	True/False
21.	Jesus able to resist all of the devil's temptations.	True/False
22.	Knowing the Scripture helped Jesus when he was tempted.	True/False
23.	Jesus had help from the angles while being tempted by the devil	True/False
24.	Did the devil ever leave Jesus?	YES/NO
25.	Did the angels come and ministered unto Jesus?	YES/NO
26.	Did all this temptation come upon Jesus before he had fast?	YES/NO
27.	Did this take place before his baptism?	YES/NO
28.	After Jesus was baptized, he offered the world's kingdom	True/False
29.	Did Jesus get baptized without the Spirit of God showing that he was the Son of the living God?	YES/NO
30.	The Spirit of God descended like a dove, and light upon Jesus.	True/False

Worksheet Answers

- Jesus was hungry and weak after fasting for 40 days and 40 nights, but he chose not to use his divine power to satisfy his natural desire for food.
- Hunger for food and eating was good, but the timing was wrong.
- Jesus was in the desert to fast, not to eat.
- Because he had given up the unlimited humanity fully, he wouldn't use his power to change the stones to bread.
- We also may be tempted to satisfy a perfectly normal desire in a wrong way or at the wrong time. If we indulge in sex before marriage or if we steal to get food, we are trying to satisfy God-given desire in wrong ways. We must remember, many of our desires are normal and good, but God wants us to satisfy them in the right way and at the right time.
- Jesus was able to resist all of the devil's temptations because he not only knew the Scripture, but he also obeyed it.

The Temptation of Jesus (Matthew 4:1-11)

[1]   *Then was Jesus led up of the Spirit into the wilderness to be tempted of the devil.*

[2]   *And when he had fasted forty days and forty nights, he was afterward hungry.*

[3]   *And when the tempter came to him, he said, If you be the Son of God, command that these stones be made bread,*

[4]   *But he answered and said,* **it is written, Man shall not live by bread a lone, but by every word that proceeds out of the mouth of God.**

[5]   *Then the devil took him up into the holy city, and sat him on a pinnacle of the temple,*

[6]   *And said unto him, If you be the Son of God, cast yourself down, for it is written, He shall give his angels charge concerning you, and in their hands they shall bear you up, lest at any time you dash your foot against a stone.*

[7]   *Jesus said unto him,* **It is written again, You shall not tempt the Lord your God.**

[8]   *Again, the devil took him up into an exceeding high mountain and showed him all The kingdoms of the world, and the glory of them;*

[9]   *And said unto him, All these things will I give you, if you will fall down and worship me.*

[10]   *Then said Jesus unto him,* **Get thee hence, Satan: for it is written, you shall worship the Lord your God, and him only shall you serve.**

[11]   *Then the devil left him, and behold, angels came and ministered unto him.*

Jesus Was Led by the Spirit

<u>Jesus Went into the Wilderness to be Tempted</u>: We as human beings are separated from God by sin and have only one person that was in the universe who was the mediator and still is and can stand between us and God and bring us together again only Jesus Christ who is both God and man.

<u>Jesus' Sacrifice Brought New Life to the People</u>: Jesus gave his life as a ransom for our sin, a ransom was the price paid to release a slave from captivity in sin; Jesus, our mediator, gave his life in exchange for ours. By his death paid the penalty for sin.

For there is one God, and one mediator between God and men, the man Jesus Christ; who himself gave the ransom for all, to be testified in due time 1-Timothy 2:5-6).

For even the Son of man came not to be ministered unto, but to minister, and to give his life a ransom for all (Mark 10:45).

<u>Evil Thoughts and Wrong Actions</u>: I don't think I have said this before, but in case I haven't this is just a good time as any; it is easy to blame others and make excuses for evil thoughts and wrong actions. I would like to give nine illustration concerning excuses.

<u>What Excuses Include</u>:
1.   it's the other person's fault,
2.   I couldn't help it,
3.   every body's doing it;
4.   it was just a mistake:
5.   nobody's perfect;
6.   the devil made me do it;
7.   I was pressured into it,
8.   I didn't know it was wrong;
9.   God is tempting me.
A person who makes excuses is trying to shift the blame from himself or herself to something or someone else, Christians on the other hand, accepts responsibility for his or her wrong, and confesses them, and then ask God through Jesus Christ for the forgiveness of them

Every man is tempted, when he is drawn away by his own lust, and enticed. Then when lust has conceived, it brings forth sin, when it is finished, bring forth death (James 1:4-5) he also can lead people to destruction.

Concerning Temptation

<u>The Crown of Life</u>: The gospel of Jesus Christ directs man to resist temptation, promising blessedness to those who do it; the gospel also directs us to pray for deliverance from exposure to temptation and from surrender to it. The Lord will not allow His people to encounter temptation beyond their Spiritual ability to resist.

1.   <u>Blessed are Those Who Endure Temptation</u>: *Blessed is the man who endures temptation: for when he is tempted, he shall receive the crown of life, which the Lord has promised to them who love him* (James 1:12).

2.   <u>Every Man Strives for Mastery of Temptation</u>: *And every man who strives for the mastery is temperate in all things. Now they do it to obtain a corruptible crown; but we are incorruptible* (l-Corinthians 1:12).

3.   <u>Pray for Deliverance</u>: *And lead us not into temptation, but deliver us from evil, for thine are the kingdom, and the power and the glory for ever Amen* (Matthew 6:13).

4.   <u>Forgive Us Our Sins</u>: *And forgive us our sins; for we also forgive everyone who is indebted to us; and lead us not into temptation; but deliver us from evil* (Luke 11:4).

Encountering Temptation

We discussed earlier strong encouragement and how the Bible gives strong encouragement to Christians today concerning temptation. I would like to refer you back to those pages to help you understand the biblical ethics of temptation. The people who are a part of the house-hold of God are going to encounter temptation beyond their Spirit-given ability to resist, so again I encourage you look at the reference which is given again.

We are in a culture filled with moral depravity and sin-inducing pressures. This is one of the reasons we are strongly encouraged that we are to recognize the culture so that we don't get caught up into these cultures of the world. Being a part of the household of God through our Lord Jesus Christ, He helps us to understand that there is no temptation that takes us but such as is common to man. He lets us know that God is faithful, who will not suffer us to be tempted above that we are able: yet at the same time, with the temptation will also make a way to escape, or make it so that we may be able to bear it. Read (Revelation 3:10) again.

Just as God rescued Lot from Sodom, he is able to do the same for us today; in the Old Testament, temptation can best be understood as testing or proving.
The context is the covenant relation of love and faithfulness between God and his people. The Lord tested Israel to prove the true nature of her faithfulness to Him. Let us look at the way God tested Abraham. This was not to trip and watch him fall, but

to deepen his capacity to obey, and also to develop his character. Just as fire refines ore to extract precious metals, God refines His people through difficult circumstances. When we are tested we can complain, or we can try to see how God is allowing us to go through so that we can learn and have the same kind of character Abraham had.

God does not tempt nor can He be tempted with or by anything. We are under a new and better covenant than Abraham and any other of the Old Testament believers. Again I give you (Revelation 3:10) (Hebrews 8:8-11). This is the new covenant God has put His law into our hearts and minds today.

Universal Obedience

Keeping God's Commandments: A charge is being given which is the same as is before to keep and do all God's commandments. Their obedience must be carefully: observe to do, this to be done in a universal matter with the regard to God as Lord, and their God, particularly with a holy fear of Him, having submission to his authority, and a dread of His wrath.

And you shall remember all the ways which the Lord your God led you these forty years in the wilderness, to humble you, and to prove you, to know what was in your heart, whether you would keep his commandments, or no (Deuteronomy 8:2).

Therefore you shall keep the commandments of the Lord your God, to walk in his ways, and to fear him (Deuteronomy 8:6).

The great advantage of being obedient which has been set before them is that they should live and multiply, and all should be well with them.

All the commandments which I command you this day shall you observe to do, that you may live, and multiply, and go in and possess the land which the Lord swore unto your fathers (Deuteronomy 8:1).

Remember All the Ways God Led Them: Looking back upon the wilderness through which God had brought them, they were to remember all the ways which God led them for those forty years in the wilderness. Now that they have become of age, and were entering upon their inheritance, they must be reminded of the discipline they had been undergoing with their God. This is time to bring it all to their remembrance.

Confirming Faith

God's Purpose is Not to Induce His People to Sin: God's purpose is not to induce His people to sin but to confirm their faith as in the case of Job, with Satan the tempter, understand, God didn't do the tempting; He lowered Satan to do the tempting.

Some seem to think God tempted Job through Satan or used him to tempt Job. If you understand what is being done, you can see that God allowed Satan to do this. Remember God asking Satan, *Have you tried my servant Job?*. God said unto Satan, do *whatever you like, but just don't touch his soul.*

Satan Had to Obtain Permission to Tempt: *The Lord said unto Satan, have you considered my servant Job, that there is none like him in the earth (Job 1:8).Satan answered the Lord, and said, does Job fear God for naught? Satan said there is a hedge about Job, Satan said that Job will curse God to his face, God said unto Satan behold that Job has it in the power of your hands.*

The point I am trying to make is that God does not tempt anyone. The Bible assumes that we will have trials and that it is possible to profit from them. The point is to not pretend to be happy when we face trials, but to have a positive outlook and to (consider it joy) because whatever we might face through the trials of life we must have a positive outlook and try and turn the hardships into times of learning.

We can't really know the depth of our character until we see how we react under pressure. It is easy to be kind to others when everything is going well. God has promised to be with us in rough times. Ask Him to give you the strength to endure difficult times in your life. In asking God's help or His strength, it must be to endure them. Then be patient; God will not leave you alone with your problems; He will stay close and help you grow.

God Does Not Tempt

God Gives Us Choices: You can't tempt God through your disobedience in a way of making Him do anything because of it. Once you disobey that puts you in a state of disobedience to His word, and once you do that, until you repent of it, you have been drawn by your own desires not being led by His word but by your understanding.

If you would like to be a follower of Jesus Christ, you must do as He has done in obeying His Father's word. The biblical teachings show that Jesus really was the Son of God, able to overcome the devil and his temptation. A person has not shown true obedience if he or she has never had an opportunity to disobey. This isn't saying that you should disobey.

We should be obedient in order to receive the blessings of God. We will be tested because of following through obedience of the teachings of Christ Jesus. Remember your convictions are only strong if you hold up under pressure!

<u>The Devil is also Called Satan</u>: The devil, also called Satan, tempted Eve in the Garden of Eden, and later he tempted Jesus in the desert. Satan is a fallen angel; he is real, not symbolic, and is constantly fighting against those who follow and obey God.

If you aren't a follower of Christ Jest, you don't have a real problem with Satan because you are his already, so there is no need of him tempting you. You are doing everything that is pleasing to him, therefore there isn't any need to tempt you.

If Jesus had given in, His mission on earth to die for our sins and to give us the opportunity to have eternal life would have been lost to us and we would not have had the opportunity to have eternal life. When temptation seems especially strong or when you think you can rationalize giving in, consider whether Satan may be trying to block God's purposes for your life or for someone else's life.

An Example to Follow When Tempted

The temptation by the devil shows us that Jesus was human, and it gave Jesus the opportunity to reaffirm God's plan for His ministry. . It also gives us an example to follow when we are tempted. Jesus' temptation was an important demonstration of His sinlessness. He would face temptation and not give in.

<u>Temptation Itself is Not Sin</u>: Jesus was tempted by the devil, but he never sinned! Although we may feel dirty after being tempted, we should remember that temptation itself is not sin. We sin when we give in and disobey God. Remember this will help us to turn away from the temptation.

<u>Jesus Tempted in the Desert</u>: Jesus wasn't tempted inside the temple or at His baptism but in the desert where He was tired, alone, and being hungry, and most vulnerable. The devil often tempts us when we are vulnerable when we are under physical or emotional stress (for example, lonely, tired, weighing big decisions, or faced with uncertainty). He also likes to tempt us through our strengths, where we are most susceptible to pride. We must guard at all times against his attacks.

<u>Where We are Most Susceptible</u>: *Then was Jesus led up of the Spirit into the wilderness to be tempted of the devil* (Luke 4:1).

And the devil said unto him, if you be the Son of God, command this stone that it be made bread (Luke 4:3).

Things Satan Focuses On
1.   physical needs and desires
2.   possessions and power
3.   prides for a similar list

But Jesus did not give in. Jesus "has been tempted in every way, just as we are yet He was without sin." He knows firsthand what we are experiencing, and He is willing and able to help us in our struggles; when we are tempted, when we think we aren't strong enough we should turn to Him for strength.

The areas the devil's temptations focused on: *Love not the world, neither the things of the things that are in the world; if any man love the world, the love of the Father is not in him* (1-John 2:15-16).

Jesus didn't give in: *For we have not an high priest which cannot be touched with the feelings of our infirmities; but was in all points tempted like as we are, yet without sin* (Hebrews 4:15).

Jesus did not prove to be a disloyal son. He did not put the Father did not put the son to a test, or was God put to a test by the son, like Israel of old. He lives "by every word that proceeds from the mouth of the Father." Jesus was able to resist all the devil's temptations because He not only knew the Scripture, but He obeyed it. Having resisted satanic temptation Himself, He is able to comfort and aid them who are followers who are tempted in similar fashion.

He is able to comfort and aid. *For in that he himself has suffered being tempted, He is able to succor them who are tempted* (Hebrews 2:18).

Christ Suffered Pain and Temptation

Knowing that Christ suffered pain and faced temptation helps us face our trials. Jesus understands our struggles because He faced them as a human being. We can trust Christ to help us survive our suffering and overcome temptation. When you face trials, go to Jesus for strength and patience. He understands your needs and is able to help.

A Great High Priest: *Since then we have a great high priest who has passed through the heavens, Jesus the Son of God, let us hold fast our confession. For we do not have a high priest who cannot sympathize with our weakness, but one who has been tempted in all things as we are, yet without sin. Let us therefore draw near with confidence to the throne of grace, that we may receive mercy and may find grace to help in time of need* (Hebrews 4:14-16).

THIS CONCLUDES THE PAGES OF TEMPTATION

ILLUSTRATION OF ADOPTION

<u>In a Theological Sense</u>:

1.   An illustration of Paul's teachings is according to the way he has put it: adoption is an act of taking voluntarily a child or people into God's family. In other words, God has adopted the believers who have accepted Christ as their Lord and savior to be the head of their life, is adopted by God to be a part of His family.

2.   Other theological writers say adoption is an act of God's grace by which sinful people are brought into His redeemed family. In the New Testament, the Greek word translated adoption literally means "placing as a son." This is a legal term that expresses the process by which a man brings another person into his family, endowing him with the status and privileges of a biological son or daughter.

In the Old Testament, adoption was never common among the Israelites. Israel was God's first born; they were God's people which He didn't have to adopt, and they were already His family. On the other hand, in the Old Testament, adoption was done by foreigners or by Jews influenced by foreign customs.

<u>Pharaoh's Daughter and Moses</u>: The Bible doesn't say if Miriam was afraid to approach the Egyptian princess, or if the princess was suspicious of the Hebrew girl. Miriam did approach the princess, who then bought the services of Miriam and her mother.

In reading Exodus, as some seem to think, Moses was not adopted by Pharaoh's daughter. According to the Scripture which is Exodus, *the daughter of Pharaoh came down to the river to wash herself; she walked along by the riverside and when she saw the child: and, the babe wept. The Bible says that she had compassion on the child, and said this is one of the Hebrews' children. She said to her sister to Pharaoh's daughter, shall I go and call a nurse of the Hebrew women, that she may nurse the child for you? And Pharaoh's daughter said to her, go and the maid went and called the child's mother. And Pharaoh's daughter said unto her, take this child away and nurse it for me, and I will give you your wages. And the woman took the child, and nursed it* (Exodus 2:5-7).

Relationship Through Adoption

<u>Roman Law</u>: Roman law required that the adopter be a male and childless; the one to be adopted had to be an independent adult, able to agree to be adopted. In the eyes of the law, the adopted one was regarded as being born again into the new family, an illustration of what happens to the believer at conversion.

The apostle Paul used this legal concept of adoption to show the believer's relationship to God's family. Though the similar ideas are found throughout the New Testament, the word adoption, used in a theological sense, it is not biblical, it's a word used by the apostle, which is only found in the writings of the apostle Paul, (Ronan 8:15,23; 9:4; 8:23).

I would like to share this little saying with you. We are no longer fearful slaves; instead, we are the Master's children. We are and have been His creation from the beginning even though we were separated from Him because of sin.

Reconciliation: Reconciliation is the process by which God and man are brought together again. The Bible teaches that God and man are alienated from one another because of God's holiness and man's sinfulness; it also says that God loves the sinner (Roman 5:8). It is impossible for Him not to judge sin (Hebrews 10:27). This isn't saying that we are not His creation because of being alienated from Him. This is the reason why reconciliation was taken by God while we were still sinners. This is also why Christ died for us.

Reconciliation is God's own completed act, something that took place before human actions such as confession, repentance, and restitution. The only point I am trying to make here, is that God does not have to adopt us into His family. We are His through His own creation. Adoption is only an illustration of a person being born again and being adopted into the family of God spiritually. This is just like the parable of the lost son, who went to his father for his portion of goods that fell to him (Luke 15:12).

Privileges and Responsibilities

Outstanding Privilege is Being Led by the Spirit: *To redeem them who were under the law that we might receive the adoption of sons. And because you are sons God has sent into your hearts, crying, Abba, Father* (Galatians 4:5-6).

God Loves Sinners: *God commands his love toward us, in that, while we were yet sinners Christ died for* us (Roman 5:8).

Waiting for the Adoption: *And not only they, but ourselves also, who have the first-fruits of the Spirit, even we ourselves groan within ourselves waiting for the adoption, to wit, the redemption of our body* (Romans 8:23).

Who are Pertaining to the Adoption: *Who are Israelites; to whom pertain the adoption, and the glory, and the covenants, and the giving of the law, And the service of God, and the promises* (Romans 9:4).

Reconciliation is God's Complete Act: And you, who were sometimes alienated and enemies in your mind by wicked works, yet now has he reconciled? In the body of his flesh through death, to present you holy and unbelievable and unreprovable in his sight:

We Have the Word of Reconciliation: *God was in Christ, reconciling the world unto himself, not imputing their trespasses unto them; and has committed unto us the word of reconciliation* (2-Corinthians 5:19).

God's Desire that None Be Lost

God knows what is best for us. God is a better judge of what we need than we are. He can make better decisions than we can for ourselves. He is a better judge than we are; we must learn how to trust Him completely in every choice we make.

God loves us, otherwise He wouldn't have sent His only beloved Son into the world to save the people of the world. The love of God is deeply rooted in the Bible. The Hebrew term "chose" refers to covenant love. Jehovah is the God who remembers and keeps His covenants in spite of the treachery of people. His faithfulness in keeping His promises proves His love for Israel and all humanity. The word "phileo" refers to tender affection, such as toward a friend or family member.

I am not lost; I am trying to show that God doesn't need to adopt us into His family because we are already His creation in Christ Jesus. We are the redeemed of God, children who have accepted God's Son; reconciled back to God. Jesus' testimony was trustworthy because He had come from heaven and was speaking of what He had seen there.

His words were the very same words of God. Your whole spiritual life depends on your answer to one question, "Who is Jesus Christ?" If you accept Jesus as only a prophet or teacher, you have to reject His teaching, for He is said to be God's Son, even God Himself.

The heartbeat of John's Gospel is the dynamic truth that Jesus Christ is God's Son, the Messiah, the Savior, who was from the beginning and will continue to live forever. This same Jesus has invited us to accept Him and live with Him eternally. When we understand who Jesus is, we are compelled to believe what He said. Jesus Christ is the ultimate redeemer; a redeemer is to get back that which is His.

Reference To Love: *The Father loved the Son, and has given all things unto his hand* (John 3:35).

A Father's Love for His Son

Because of this unity with God, Jesus lived as God wanted Him to live. Because of our identification with Jesus, we must honor and live as He would have us to live. So the question is asked again, "Who is Jesus Christ?" In having our identification with Jesus, the questions, "What would Jesus do?" and "What would Jesus have you to do?" would help make the right choices.

The Father Loves the Son: *For the Father loves the Son, and has shown him all things that himself do: and he will show him greater works than these that you may marvel* (John 5:20).

I have gotten a little away from adoption, but I think it is good because this is giving you a little more and better understanding about the Father and Son. These who read the life of Christ are faced with one unavoidable question, "Was Jesus God? Part of any reasonable conclusion has to include the fact that He did claim to be God. We have no other choice but to agree or disagree with His claim. Eternal life is at stake in the choice.

CHART: The Claims of Christ

1. Jesus claimed to be the fulfillment of the Old Testament Prophecies:
   - Matthew 5:17; 14:33; 16:16-17; 26:31, 53-56; 27:43
   - Mark 14:21, 61-62
   - Luke 4:16-21; 7:18-23; 18:31; 22:37; 24:44
   - John 2:22; 5:45-47; 6:45; 7:40; 10:34-36; 13:18; 1525; 20:9

2. The Son of Man:
   - Matthew 8:20; 12:8; 19:28' 20:18-19; 24:27, 44; 25:31; 26:2,45, 064

3. The Son of God:
   - Matthew 23:9-10; 26:63-64
   - Mark 3:11-12; 14:61-62
   - Luke 8:28; 10:22
   - John 1:18; 3:35-36; 5:1826; 5:40; 10:36; 11:4; 17:1; 19:7

4. The Messiah the Christ:
   - Matthew 23:9-10; 26:63-64
   - Mark 8:29-30
   - Luke 4:41;23:1-2; 24:25-27
   - John 4:25-26; 10:24-25; 11:27

5. Teacher / Master:
   - Matthew 26:18; John 13:13-14

6. One with Authority to Forgive:
   - Mark 2:1-12;
   - Luke 7:48-48)

7. Lord:
   - Mark 5:19
   - John 13:13-14; 20:28

8. Savior:
   - Luke 19:10

- John 3:17; 10:9

This concludes the Chart of the Claims of Christ

<u>Jesus Talks About Love</u>: Jesus is talking about a new relationship between the believer and God. It is showing the love in the family between not only the Father and Son, but the believer as well. People approached God through priests; however, after Jesus' resurrection, any believer could approach God directly. A new day has dawned and now all believers are priests, talking with God personally and directly.

We approach God, not because of our own merit, but because Jesus is our great high priest, and made us acceptable to God.

For the Father himself loves you, because you have loved me, and have believed that I came out from God (John 16:27).

Having therefore, brethren, boldness to enter into the holiest by the blood of Jesus, by a new and living way, which he has consecrated for us, through the veil, that is to say, his flesh; and having a high priest over the house of God; Let us draw near with a true heart in full assurance of faith, having our hearts sprinkled from an evil conscience, and our bodies washed with pure water. Let us hold fast the profession of our faith without wavering; for he is faithful that promised (Hebrews 10:19-23).

From Argument to Instruction

<u>The Superiority of Faith</u>: The author writing Hebrews cites may examples of those who have demonstrated faith throughout their history. Living by faith is far better than merely fulfilling rituals and rules. This saying is according to the Hebrews; this can challenge us to grow in faith and to live in obedience to God's law each day (Hebrews 10:19-13:25)

<u>The Living Way Consecrated for the Believer</u>: The most Holy Place in the temple was sealed from the view of curtain. I encourage you to read (Hebrews 10:19-20). Only the high priest could enter this holy room, and he did so only once a year on the Day of (Atonement) when he offered the sacrifice for the (nation's sins).
But Jesus' death removed the curtain, and all believers may walk into God's presence at any time (Hebrews 6:19-20).you can refer back to page 53 in reading Hebrews 10:19-23.

<u>Concerning Death Removing the Curtain</u>: *Having therefore, brethren, boldness to enter into the holiest by the blood of Jesus, by a new and living way, which he has consecrated for us, through the veil, that is to say, his flesh* (Hebrews 6:19-20).

Understanding the Consecrating Reasons

Because it was upon this the performance of this undertaking for our redemption and salvation did depend upon His death and resurrection. If He had not given His life a ransom, and had not resumed it, it does not appear that His giving it would have been accepted as a satisfaction. If He be imprisoned for our debt, and lie by it, we are undone.

Christ Being Raised from the Dead: *Then she ran and came to Simon Peter and to the other disciple whom Jesus loved, and said unto them, they have taken away the Lord out of the sepulcher and we know not where they have laid him* (John 20:2).

A Life Undone: *And if Christ be not raised, your faith is vain; You are yet in your sin* (1-Corinthians 15:17).

Being Undone

If Christ Had Not Been Raised: Because Jesus never showed Himself alive after His resurrection to all the people, we should have said, and I did say we, but rather they should have said, "Let His knowledge of death be private, and His glorious resurrection lie in public."

But God's thoughts are not as ours and He ordered it that His death should be public before the sun, by the same token that the sun blushed and hid his face upon it. But the demonstration of His resurrection should be reserved as a favor for His particular friends, and by them to be published to the world, that those might be blessed who have not seen, and yet have believed.

God Raised Up Jesus on the Third Day: *Him God raised up on the third day and showed him openly, not to all the people, but unto witnesses chosen before of God, even to us, who did eat and drink with him after he rose from the dead* (Acts 10:40-41). We have in this verse the first step towards the proof of Christ's resurrection which is, that the sepulcher was found empty.

The Aspect of God's Love: In all that has been read concerning the aspect of God's love that caused Him to help the most miserable, just as grace is the aspect of His love that moves Him to forgive the guilty. In most cases, those who are miserable may be so either because of breaking God's law or because of circumstance beyond their control. This is something to think about when dawn into temptation. It is true that God's mercy on the miserable sometimes extends beyond punishment. He loved us even when we were still in sin. This not saying that we are getting away with sin because we are not (Ephesians 2:4- 6). We talked about this some before. (We will get back into the adoption on the next page)

Christ the Ultimate Redeemer

The Greek word for redeemer is not used. Jesus gave His life as a ransom for many. Even today we must learn to serve others as Jesus did; this is what the Christian walk is all about--being a servant of God through Jesus Christ.

James and John wanted the highest position Jesus had to offer which was being in His kingdom. But Jesus told them true greatness comes in serving others. Peter who was one of the disciples heard this message and expands the thought of it in (1-Peter 5:1-4) in saying, *the elders which are among you I exhort, who also an elder, and a witness of the suffering of Christ, and also a partaker of the glory that shall be revealed. Freed the flock of God which is among you, taking the oversight thereof, not by constraint, but willingly; not for filthy lucre, but of a ready mind; Neither as being lords over God's heritage, but being ensamples to the flock, And when the chief Shepherd shall appear, you shall receive a crown of glory that fad not away.*

Even the Son of man came not to be ministered unto, But to minister, and give his life a ransom for many (Mark 10:45)

This verse reveals not only the motive for Jesus' ministry, but also the basis for our salvation. A ransom was the price paid to release a slave like me. Jesus paid a ransom for us because we could not pay it for ourselves. His death released all of us from our slavery to sin.

The disciples thought Jesus' life and power would save them from Roman rule. Jesus said His death would save them from sin, an even greater slavery than the Rome. We can read more about the ransom Jesus paid for us is in (1-Peter 1:18-19).

Saved by the Precious Blood

A Redeemed Slave: A slave was "redeemed" when someone paid money to buy his or her freedom. God redeemed us from the substance of sin, not with money, but with the precious blood of his own Son. We cannot escape from sin on our own; only the life of God's Son freed us.

Our Old Life is Crucified: *Knowing this that our old life is crucified with him, that the body of sin might be destroyed, that henceforth we should not serve sin. For he who is dead is freed from sin* (Romans 6:6-7).

For You are Bought with a Price: *For you are bought with a price: therefore glorify God in your body, and in your spirit, which is God's through Jesus Christ* (1-Corinthians 6:20).

<u>Being Dead in Your Sin</u>: *And you, being dead in your sins and the uncircumcision of your flesh, has he quickened together with him, having forgiven you all trespasses blotting out the handwriting of ordinance that was against us, which was contrary to us, and took it out of the way, nailing it to the cross* (Colossians 2:13-14).

<u>He Entered Once into the Holy Place</u>: *Neither by the blood of goats and calves, but by his own blood he entered in once into the holy place, having obtained eternal redemption for us* (Hebrews 9:12).

How can we escape such a great of salvation, it is by his precious Blood we are saved, if it wasn't for the mercy and the grace of God through Jesus Christ, we would still be in slave.

(This concludes the five references)

WORKSHEET: Peter's Confession of Faith

Answers to Worksheet

On this page are the answers to the questions that will be ask on the next page. In this page will be Bible verses taken from Matthew 16:16-19. Verse 15 is the question Jesus the disciples. Verse 16 is the confession of Peter's faith which will be the questions for you to be able to get your answer from 16-19.

Who Say You That I Am? (Matthew 16:16-19).
[16] And Simon Peter answered and said, you are the Christ, the Son of the living God.
*[17] And Jesus answered and said unto him, **Blessed art you, Simon Barjona; for flesh and blood has not revealed it unto you, but my Father who is in heaven.***
*[18] **And I say also unto you, that you are Peter, and upon this rock I will build my church; and the gates of hell shall not prevail against it.***
*[19] **And I will give unto you the keys of the kingdom of heaven; and whatsoever you shall bind on earth shall be bound in heaven; and whatsoever you shall loose on earth shall be loosed in heaven** (Matthew 16:16-19).*

The Unity of the Spirit

We Are One Body of the Church: The same applies for this as that of Peter's confession; you have here Ephesians 4:11-16.

[11] And he gave some, apostles; and some, prophets; and some, evangelists; and some, pastor and teachers; [12] For the perfecting of the saints, for the work of the ministry, for the edifying of the body of Christ; [13] Until we all come in the unity of the faith, and of the knowledge of the Son of God, unto a perfect man, unto the measure of the stature of the fullness of Christ; [14] That we henceforth be no more children, tossed to and fro, and carried about with every wind of doctrine, by the sleight of men, and cunning craftiness, whereby they lie in wait to deceive; [15] But speaking the truth in love, may grow up into him in all things, which is the head even Christ; [16] From whom the whole body fitly joined together and compacted by that which every joint supplies, according to the effectual working in the measure of every part, makes increase of the body unto the edifying of itself in love (Ephesians 4:11-16).

[19] Now therefore you are no more strangers and foreigners, but fellow-citizens with the saints, and of the household of God; [20] And are built upon the foundation of the apostles and prophets, Jesus Christ himself being the chief corner stone; [21] In whom all the building fitly framed together growth unto a holy temple in the Lord; [22] In whom you also are built together for an habitation of God through the Spirit (Ephesians 2:19-22).

WORKSHEET:

These questions and answers are according to Matthew 15:19; Ephesians 4:11-16; and Ephesians 2:19-22. If you don't know the answers, I encourage you to read these three chapters, try to answer the questions before reading that is to see how well you know the Bible.

EPHESIANS 2:19-22		
1.	Ephesians 2:19 says, *You are no more strangers and foreigners, but fellow-citizens.*	True / False
2.	Ephesians 2:21 says, *In whom all the building fitly framed together grow unto a holy place to the Lord.*	True / False
3.	Ephesians 2:20 says, *The foundation of the apostles and prophets, Jesus Christ being the chief cornerstone.*	True / False
4.	Ephesians 2 Verse _____ says, *For an habitation of God through the Spirit.*	19 / 20
EPHESIANS 4:11-16		
5.	Ephesians 4:11 says, *He gave some, apostles; ;and some, prophets; and some, evangelists.*	True / False
6.	Ephesians 4:14 says, *Be no more children, tossed to and fro*	True / False
7.	Ephesians 4:12 says, *For the perfecting of the saints, for the work of the ministry*	True / False
8.	Ephesians 4:13 says, *Until we all come in the unity of the faith, and of the knowledge of the Son of God*	True / False
9.	Ephesians 4:15 says, *Speaking the truth in love*	True / False
10.	Ephesians 4:17 says, *This I say therefore, and testify in the Lord*	True / False
11.	Ephesians 4:16 says, *The whole body fitly joined together*	True / False
MATTHEW 16:13-19		
12.	In Matthew 16:15 Jesus asked Peter, Who do men say that I am?	True / False
13.	Jesus blessed Peter for his confession of faith.	True / False
14.	After Peter's confession, Jesus said, ***You are Peter***	True / False
15.	In Matthew 16:19 Jesus said that he would give Peter the keys of the kingdom.	True / False
16.	Jesus said to Peter that flesh and blood did not reveal his confession to him.	True / False
17.	In Matthew 16:18 Jesus told Peter that he would build his church upon this rock.	True / False

WORKSHEET: Marriage and Family

<u>It is Not Good Man Should be Alone</u>: *The Lord God said, it is not good that man should be alone; I will make him a help meet* (Genesis 2:18).

1.	The woman was made for the man	True / False
2.	The man was lonely in the Garden of Eden	True / False
3.	In the Garden of Eden God placed the man	True / False
4.	In Genesis after the time of God's creation, he saw something that was not good. Explain:	
5.	God made the man for the woman	True / False
SPIRITUALLY FROM A THEOLOGICAL POINT		
6.	Genesis 2:23: Because God saw that man was lonely he made him a help meet. This is pertaining to a wife ethically speaking, however, biblically, Adam said, this is now bone of my bone, and flesh of my flesh: she shall be called woman because she was taken out of man	
7.	Should a man leave his father and mother for his wife	Yes / No
8.	Do you find that to be meet toward his wife	True / False
9.	Is this showing love for his wife	Yes / No
10.	(Ephesians 5:33) says, Nevertheless let every one of you in particular so love his wife even as himself; and the wife see tat she reverence her husband	True / False
11.	When the question is asked concerning God making Adam a help meet and they should ask the meaning of it you can say she is to love and care for her husband, for the meet shall help the other that is overtaken in a fault	True / False
12.	Should that be the case, you that which are spiritual, should restore such a one in the spirit of meekness	True / False
13.	Should you consider yourself lest you be also tempted	True / False

Throughout the Bible you will read concerning meet, meekness, is concerning love and caring for another. That is what God is all about, loving and caring for His children who love and obey Him; just as we are to be to our wife, and the wife is to be toward her husband.

Conforming Moral Standards of Husband and Wife

Ecclesiastes takes up where God said it is not good that man should be alone. The Ecclesiastes gives its reason why it isn't good that man should be alone, by saying two are better than one; because they have a good reward for their labor. It also says, *if they fall, the one will lift up his fellow: but woe to him who is alone when he fall; for he has not another to help him up* (Ecclesiastes 4:9-10).

<u>In Sorrow You Shall Bring Forth Children</u>: In Genesis we can see and understand Ecclesiastes' sayings concerning the needs of the two people. In this case I will say husband and wife as God had planned it according to Genesis where he said unto the woman, *I will greatly multiply your sorrow and your conception; in sorrow shall bring forth children; and your desire shall be to your husband, and he shall rule over you* (Genesis 3:16).

<u>I Will Make You a Help Meet</u>: In making a help meet for Adam, it was to be of the same nature and the same rank of being; a helper near him, one to cohabit with him, and to be always at his side or at hand; a help before hand, one that he should look upon with pleasure and delight. In our best state in this world we have need of one another, for we are members one of another and the eye cannot say to the other I have no need of you. According to 1-Corinthians 12:21, *The eye cannot say unto the hand, I have no need of you: nor again the head to the feet, I have no need of you.*

God has tempered the body together, having given more abundant honor to that there should be no schism in the body; but that the members should have the same care one for another (1-Corinthians 12:24-25).

We therefore should be glad to receive help from others, and be willing to give help as there is the occasion. It is God only who perfectly knows our needs and is perfectly able to supply them all. Philippians 4:19 says, *But my God shall supply all your needs according to his riches in glory by Christ Jesus*; in Him alone our help is and from Him is our helper. A suitable wife is a help meet and is from the Lord.

Caring for the World

<u>Caring for the Things of the World</u>: For the Christians it is likely to be comfortable when meekness dissects and determines the choice, and mutual helpless is the constant of care and endeavor. The Bible teaches the difference between the wife and the virgin. He who is married cares for the things of the world. That is, how he is to please his wife. It talks also about the difference between the wife and a virgin. An unmarried person cares for the things of God, that they may be holy in both, body and in spirit: but he who is married cares for the things of the world, which is how to please the husband and the wife (1-Corinthians 7:33-34).

<u>Words of Encouragement</u>: Our Lord Jesus Christ, having proved himself able to save, and here He is showing Himself as willing as He is able to save. We suppose the prophet Isaiah to say something of himself in these verses, in a way of encouraging himself to go on in his work as a prophet, notwithstanding the many hardships he met with, not doubting but that God would stand by him and strengthen him. Like David he speaks of himself as a type of Christ, who is here prophesied of and promised to be the Savior.

I could not think of any better words to share with a marriage that is going through and having doubts about staying together when things of life get you to a point you think there is no strength to go on, just think of what our Lord Jesus went through to see that you can make, and how the prophet Isaiah was encouraged in accepting the job that was put before him.

An Acceptable Preacher

As an acceptable preacher, Isaiah, a prophet, was qualified for the work to which he was called. So were the rest of God's prophets, and others whom He employed as His messengers. This isn't only saying His messengers, but if He has joined you together as husband and wife, this should mean just as much as it was to the prophet Isaiah being the preacher that he was. He was qualified just as you were qualified to say, "I will and unto death do I part," and likewise said she, "Until death do I part." This is to him and her, her and him, not to him and him any more than it means to her and her. When God said it is not good that man should be alone, he didn't mean that he should have another man for a help meet.

<u>Qualified for the Work of God</u>: Having the knowledge of which you are called, by God in he has employed you as his messenger; there is one thing for sure, God dose not employ anyone who have desires for the same sex and committees to it. Nor will he employ a foolish person as his messenger.

When God created man, he made woman as man's help meet which is saying the desire were met to be for each other, male and female, the female's desires were to be for her husband and not for another woman, she was to bring forth children and because of that, she will greatly receive or have sorrow and her conception; in sorrow (Genesis 3:16) there is no room in God's righteousness for homo sexual persons.

The tongue of a learned person in the Lord Jesus Christ, knows how to give instruction, how to speak a word in season to him that is weary, God wakes us each day that we see, he waken us each morning by morning, with a ear to as that we have learned to speak to the weary.

Having a Tongue of the Learned

A Tongue of the Learned: *The Lord God has given me the tongue of the learned, that I should know how to speak a word in season to him that is weary: he wakens morning by morning, he wakens mine ear to hear as the learned* (Isaiah 50:4).

God gives us things of yesterday for our learning today, when we see the conviction of Pharaoh after Moses were given instruction to speak a word in season which was the word of learned to speak for the terror and conviction of Pharaoh.

Who Has Made Man's Mouth? *And the Lord said unto him, who has made man's mouth? Or who made the dumb, or deaf, or the seeing, or the blind? Have not I the Lord? Now therefore go, and I will be with your mouth, and teach you what you shall say* (Exodus 4:11-12).

He Gave to Christ the Tongue of the Learned: God gave Christ the tongue of the learned, to speak a word in season for the comfort of those who are weary and heavily laden under the burden of sin, Grace was poured into his lips and they are said to drop sweet smelling myrrh.

Words to the Weary: *Come unto me all you that labor and are heavy laden, and I will give you rest. Take my yoke upon you, and learn of me; for I am meek and lowly in heart: and you shall find rest unto your soul. For my yoke is easy, and my burden is light* (Matthew 11:28-29).

Relation to Husband and Wife: Some single people feel tremendous pressure to be married. There are some who think their lives can be complete only with a spouse. Paul underlines one advantage of being single and that is having a greater focus on Christ and His work. If you are unmarried, you can use your special opportunity to serve Christ wholeheartedly.

Advantage of Being Single: *But he who is married care for the things that are of the world, how he may please his wife* (1-Corinthians 7:33).*There is difference also between a wife and a virgin. The unmarried woman cares for the things of the Lord, that she may be holy both in body and in spirit: but she who is married cares for the things of the world, how she may please her husband* (1-Corinthians 7:34).

A Social Family

A Companionship as a Couple: A companion, of or two people living their lives together and dealing with one another: as, is a social problem, living this way: looking at a father from a social point of view, the father's responsibility was or is to see that no one takes advantage of any member of his family. Those who were not protected by a father were truly disadvantaged persons. The two most common basic concepts into which knowledge is classified, (social) or (spiritual)."fatherless" people were widows and orphans.

The Father's Responsibility

There are four specific duties of a father toward his son, as stated in the Jewish writings:
1.   to have the son circumcised;
2.   to pass on his inheritance to his firstborn son;
3.   to find his son a wife; and
4.   to teach him a trade.
This is from a social way of life.

The Spiritual Concepts of Life: First of all, the father was responsible for the spiritual well-being of the family, as well as the individual members of the family. In the earliest ages, the father functioned as the priest of his family, sacrificing on their behalf.

In reading about Abram, one would have expected Abram having had such an extraordinary call to Canaan some great event should have followed upon his arrival there, it seems that he would have been introduced with all possible marks of honor and respect, and that the kings of Canaan should immediately have surrendered their crowns to him, and done him homage. Rather he comes not with observation, and little notice is taken of him, still God will have him to live by faith.

Living By Faith: And he removed from hence unto a mountain on the east of Bethel, And pitched his tent, having Bethel on the West, and Hai on the east:
And there he build an altar unto the Lord, and called upon the Name of the Lord (Genesis 12:8).I encourage you to read verses 6-7-9.

Later, when priesthood was established in Israel and the layman no longer functioned at an altar, the father's spiritual role was redefined. He continued to be the religious leader in the home. This involved the training of the children in godliness.

A Biblical Illustration: Job showed deep concern for the spiritual welfare of his children. He was fearful that they might have sinned unknowingly, so, he offered sacrifices for them. Parents today can show the same concern by praying for their children. Under the new convent, the soul that sins is the soul that dies. If someone sins willingly and knowingly, there is no need of praying for that child. Yes, you can ask God's mercy upon that child, but that is as far as you can go with that. Job would make "sacrifices" each day to ask God to forgive them, to help them grow, to protect them, and to help them please Him.

When you are obedience to his word as he has asked, he will protect and led you according to his will, it is said, to trust in the Lord with all your heart, and lean not unto your understanding: in all your ways acknowledge him, and he hall direct your paths (Proverbs 3:S-6).there is another saying to help, let not mercy and truth forsake you bind them about your neck; write them upon the table of your heart: so shall you find favor and good understanding in the sight of God and man (Proverbs 3:3-4).And the times of this ignorance God winked at; but now command all men everywhere to repent: because he had appointed a day, in the which he will judge the world in righteousness by that man whom he have ordained; whereof he had given assurance unto all men, in that he raised him from the dead (Acts 17:30-31).

<u>Sanctified for His Children</u>: *And it was so, when the days of their feasting were gone about, then Job sent and sanctified them and rose up early in the morning, and offered burnt offerings according to the number of them all: for Job said, It may be that my sons have sinned, and cursed God in their hearts. This did Job continually* (Job 1:5).

Training Up a Child

<u>Parents Who Make All the Choices</u>: Parents who like to make all the choices for their child sometimes hurt the child in the long run. When parents teach a child how to make decisions, they don't have to watch every step the child takes. They know their children will remain on the right path because they have made the choice themselves. Train your children to choose the right way. As the Bible teaches, *you fathers are not to provoke your children to wrath* according to (Ephesians 6:4). *Train up a child in the way he should go* (Proverbs 22:6). This should be the responsibility of a father whether it is socially or spiritually, he should be concept into which knowledge is classified as spiritual teaching.

<u>Train Up a Child in the Way He Should Go</u>: The purpose of parental discipline is to help children grow, not to exasperate and provoke them to anger or discouragement. Parenting is not easy it takes lots of patience to raise children in a loving, Christian home, in a Christ-honoring manner. (Proverbs 6:4).

Frustration and anger should not be causes for discipline. Instead, parents should act in love, treating their children as Jesus treats the people He loved. This is vital to children's development and to their understanding of what Christ is like;

You fathers, provoke not your children to wrath but bring them up in the nurture and admonition of the Lord (Ephesians 6:4).

Classification of a Father

Responsibility along with the honor of the position as head of the family, the father was expected to assume certain responsibilities. These responsibilities can be classified into three Categories: spiritual, social, and economic.

Economic Responsibility

<u>Fathers are to Provide Economically</u>: Economically, fathers are to provide for the needs of the various members of his family. From time to time there is a lazy person who fails to provide for his family. There was a way of shaming him, in which the conscientious man seeks to mock the lazy man, to shame him to do what is expected of him.

Go to the ant, you sluggard; consider her ways, and be wise: which have no guide, overseer, or ruler, Provident her meat in the summer, and gathered her food in the harvest. How long will you sleep, you sluggard? When will you arise out of your sleep? Yet a little sleep, a little slumber, a little folding of the hands to sleep: so shall your poverty come as one that traveled, and you want as an armed man (Proverbs 6:6-11).

The apostle Paul rebuked those who considered themselves Christian who did not look after the needs of their families. Everyone has relatives, family of some kind. Family relationships are important in God's eyes; those who neglect their family responsibilities have denied the faith. Are you doing your part to meet the needs of those included in your family circle?

<u>If any Provide not for His Own</u>: *If any provide not for his own and especially for those of his own house, he has denied the faith, and is worse than an infidel* (1-Timothy 5:8).

God Illustrated Marriage for Us

God illustrated for us that in marriage man and woman symbolically become one flesh. This is a mystical union of a couple's heart and lives. Many couples find it difficult to accept. According to Genesis 2:24, *Therefore shall a man leave his father and his mother, and shall cleave unto his wife: and they shall be one flesh.*

Throughout the Bible, God treats this special partnership very seriously. If you are married or planning to be married, I will ask the question again, "Are you willing to keep the commitment that makes the two of you one?" This goal in marriage should be more than friendship.

God forms and equips men and women for a task that leads to two goals, that is to honor him and to give life to the woman who then gives life to the world and Christ gives eternal spiritual life. Each role carries exclusive privileges; there is no room for thinking that one sex is more superior to the other. The wife is to honor her husband and the husband is to love his wife as Christ loved the church.

<u>Wife Honor Your Husband</u>: Wives, submit yourselves unto your own husbands, as unto the Lord (Ephesians 5:22).

<u>Love the Wife as Christ Loved the Church</u>: *Husbands, love your wives, even as Christ also loved the church, and gave himself for it; that he might sanctify and cleanse it with the washing of water by the word, that he might present it to himself a glorious church, not having sport, or wrinkle, or any such thing, but that it should be holy and without blemish. So ought men to love their wives as their own bodies. He who loves his wife loves himself* (Ephesians 5:23-28).

Submitted to His Will

<u>Christ Submitted His Will to the Father</u>: At whose name "every knee should bow, in heaven and on earth" (Philippians 2:10), submitted his will to the Father, and we must honor Christ by following his example. When we submit to God, we become more willing to obey His command to submit to others that is to subordinate our rights to theirs.

In a marriage relationship, both husband and wife are called to submit. For the wife, this means willingly following her husband's leadership in Christ. For the husband, it means to put aside his own interests in order to care for his wife.

Submission is really a problem in homes and sometimes on our job, where both partners have a strong relationship with Christ and where each is concerned for the happiness of the other; but, it is said that one must honor the one that has rule over you, all that is saying, submitted to the one with the authority.

In Paul's days, woman, children, and slaves were to submit to the head of the family. Slaves would submit until they were freed; male children would be until they grew up; and women and girls were to submit throughout their whole lives.

It seems that Paul emphasized the quality of all believers in Christ should be submitted to the teachings of Christ and follow his example of living. The emphasis is that *there is neither Jew nor Greek, bond nor free, male nor female, for all are one in Christ Jesus* (Galatians 3:28). This didn't suggest overthrowing the Roman society to achieve getting his message over as some of us do today in order to please the hears. Instead, he counseled all believers to submit to one another by choosing to talk about the husband and wife. This kind of mutual submission preserves order and harmony in the family while it increases love and respect among family members. Amen.

Teaching on Submission

<u>According to the Bible</u>: The man is the spiritual head of the family, and his wife

should acknowledge his leadership. Real spiritual leadership involves service. Just as Christ served the disciples, even to the point of washing their feet, so the husband is to serve his wife.

Master and Lord: *You call me Master and Lord: and you say well; for so I am; If I then, your Lord and Master, have washed your feet; you also ought to wash one another's feet. For I have given you an example, that you should do as I have done unto you* (John 13:13-15).

Husbands should not take the advantage of the leadership role, and a wise and Christ-honoring wife will not try to undermine her husband' leadership. Either approach causes disunity and friction in marriage.

I am going to use the word "perhaps" because I am not quite sure if these sayings are true or not, so I will say perhaps. Why did Paul tell the wives to submit and the husbands to love? Perhaps Christian women in the early days newly freed in Christ found submission difficult; perhaps Christian men, used to the Roman custom of giving unlimited power to the head of the family, were not treating their wives with respect and love. Yes, of course both husband and wives should submit to each other, just as both should love each other.

Therefore as the church is subject unto Christ, so let the wives be to their husbands in everything (Ephesians 5:24).

Submitting yourselves one to another in the fear of God (Ephesians 5:21).

The Family of God

God Instituted the Family: From this study I learned the Biblical writers used other analogies from the family to describe various aspects of the gospel. Adoption is a comparable word which is used to describe the aspects of believers to be brought into the family of God's house.

The believer must be "born from above" or "born again." A person has God as his father and must realize that other believers are also a part of the family of the household of God. Being a part of the family, he is our "father," "mother," "brother," and "sister." This makes up the family in the house hole of God.

Except a Man is Born Again: *[3] Jesus answered and said unto him, Verily, verily, I say unto you, except a man be born again, he cannot see the kingdom of God;, [5] Jesus answered, Verily, verily, I say unto you, except a man be born of water and of the Spirit, he cannot enter into the kingdom of God* (John 3:3, 5).

The Family of God: *Rebuke not an elder, but entreat him as father; and the younger men as brethren; the elder women as mothers; the younger as sisters, with all purity* (1-Timothy 5:1-2).

The body of believers is known as the church which is referred to as the "household of God"

The Household of God: *Now therefore you are no more strangers and foreigners, but fellow-citizens with the saints, and of the house-hold of God* (Ephesians 2:19).

The Kingdom of God

What is the Kingdom of God? What did Nicodemus know about the kingdom? From the biblical aspect he knew it would be ruled by God, it would be restored on earth, and it would incorporate God's people. Jesus revealed to this devout Pharisee that the kingdom would come to the whole world. Not just the Jews, but Nicodemus would or could be a part of it, if he would personally be born again (John 3:5).

The Concept of Kingdom: The kingdom is personal, not national or ethnic, and its entrance requirements are repentance and spiritual rebirth.

You have read of the devout Pharisee. Jesus later taught that God's kingdom had already begun in the hearts of believers.

Neither shall they say, Lo here! Or, Lo there! For, behold, the kingdom of God is within you (Luke 17:21). It will be fully realized when Jesus returns again to judge the world and abolish evil forever (Revelation 21 and 22).

The Household of Faith: *As we have therefore opportunity, let us do well unto all men, especially unto them who are of the household of faith* (Galatians 6: 10).

In addition, the concepts of adoption are used to describe the position of believers in God's family (Galatians 4:5).(l-Peter 1:4).

To redeem them who were under the law that we might receive the adoption of sons (Galatians 4:5).

To an inheritance incorruptible, and undefiled, and that fade not away, reserved in heaven for you (1-Peter 1:4).

In the Family of God

We are Referred to as the Church of God: The term redeemer is used of God to express His intimate relationship with His people. The scope of this verse, "fear not," is to silence the fear, and encourage the faith, of the servants of God in their distresses.

<u>Fear Not, You Worm Jacob</u>: Fear not, you worm Jacob, and you men of Israel; I will help you, said the Lord, and your redeemer, the Holy One of Israel (Isaiah 41: 14).

God is their "next of kin" who ransoms them from bondage. He pays the price to set them free. The biblical teachings help believers understand today that God has bought us at a price; therefore, we are to glorify Him. This verse ends with God's sorrow over the spiritual decay of His people. Ethically speaking, God is saying today, despite of the people's spiritual failure, He will show them mercy, bring them back from captivity, and restore them.

<u>God's Next of Kin</u>: *But now this is what the Lord that created you, Oh Jacob, and He who formed you, Oh Israel, Fear not: for I have redeemed you, I have called you by your name; you are mine. When you pass through the water, I will be with you; and through the river, they shall not overflow you. When you walk through the fire you shall not be burned; neither shall the flame kindle upon you. For I am the Lord your God, the Holy One of Israel, and your Savior: I gave Egypt for your ransom, Ethiopia and Saba for you* (Isaiah 43:1-3).

God will do the same today that He has done then, because we accepted His Son as Lord of our life and He is our heavenly Father. He will give us an outpouring of love, and then the world would know that God alone has done this because of His love and mercy for them who love and obey.

God's Family

<u>As the Body of Christ</u>: Many of the people today say and believe that they have the right to do what they want with their own bodies. Although they may think that because of having the freedom, they are really enslaved to their desires. When we become Christians, the Holy Spirit fills and lives in us; therefore we no longer own our bodies as we may think. We have been "bought at a price" refers to being from slaves from sin, and being purchased at auction. Christ's death freed us from sin and obligates us to His service. If you live in a building owned by someone else, you try not to violate the building's rules. Because your body belongs to God, you must not violate His standards for living.

<u>Do Not Violate God's Temple</u>: *What? Know you not that your body is the temple of the Holy Ghost which is in you, which you have of God, and you are not your own? For you are bought with a price: therefore glorify God in your body, and in your spirit, which is God's body?* (1-Corinthians 6:19-20).

<u>God Knows His Children</u>: From this background we can more fully appreciate God as the believer's father. He knows all about His children, even the numbering of the hairs on their head. Jesus said that God is also aware of everything that happens even to sparrows, and

you are far more valuable to him than they are.

But the very hairs of your head are all numbered (Matthew 10:30).

The Value of God's Family

He Protects His Family: God protects his children and rescues them when they gets into trouble, he teaches them the way that they should go and supplies all of their needs, in return, the father expects honor from his children, although he does not receive it. Jesus sought to instill reverence and honor in the disciples when He taught them to pray: in saying: "our Father in heaven"

When He Gets In Trouble: (Isaiah 63:15-16)

He Teaches Them the Way that they Should Go: (Hosea 11:1-3)

He Supplies All Their Needs: Matthew 6:33

The Father Expects Honor from His Children: (Malachi 1:6)

The People of the World: We are so valuable that God sent His only Son to die for us (John 3:16). Because God places such value on us, we need never fear personal threats or difficult trials. These can't shake God's love or dislodge His Spirit from within us. This doesn't mean that God will take away all our troubles (Matthew 10: 16). The real test of value is how well something holds up under the wear, tear, and abuse of everyday life. Those who stand up for Christ in spite of their troubles truly have lasting value and will receive great rewards (Matthew 5:11-12).

So again, you are not to fear therefore, you are of more value than many sparrows (Matthew 10:31).

The Birth of Christ (Matthew 1:18-19)

In a Marriage the Two Must Agree to the Union: After the agreement, there should be announcement be made, at this point, the couple is "pledged." This shows that there is a relationship.

This relationship can be broken only through death or divorce. With Joseph and Mary sexual relations were not permitted before marriage nor was it permitted to a divorce unless there was sex with someone before or during those relations in marriage.

When we look at Joseph and Mary's relationship, they were engaged. Mary seemed to have been unfaithful to Joseph. According to the Jewish civil law, Joseph had a right to divorce her. The Jewish authorities could have had her stoned to death (Deuteronomy 22:23-

24).

So the question is, Why is the virgin birth important to the Christian faith? Jesus Christ had to be free from the sinful nature which passed through other human beings by Adam. Because Jesus was born of a woman, he was a human being; but as the Son of God, Jesus was born without any sin. He was both fully human and fully divine.

Because Jesus lived as a man, we know that He fully understands our experiences and struggles (Hebrews 4:15-16). Because He is God, He has the power and authority to deliver us from sin (l-Colossians 2:13-15). We can tell Jesus all our thoughts, feelings, and needs. He has been where we are now, and he has the ability to help.

<u>Could Have had her Stoned to Death</u>: *If a damsel that is a virgin be betrothed unto a husband, and a man find her in the city and lie with her; then you shall bring them both out unto the gate of that city, and you shall stone them with stones that they die; the damsel because she cried not, being in the city; and the man because he has humbled his neighbor's wife: so you shall put away evil from among you.*

Jesus Lived as a Man

<u>Jesus Understands Our Experiences</u>: *For we have not a high priest who cannot be touched with the feeling of our infirmities; but was in all points tempted like as we are, yet without sin; Let us therefore come boldly unto the throne of grace, that we may obtain mercy, and find grace to help in time of need* (Hebrews 4:15-16).

<u>God Has the Power and Authority to Deliver</u>: *And you, being dead in your sins and the uncircumcision of your flesh, has he quickened together with him, having forgiven you all trespass; blotting out the handwriting of ordinance that was against us, which was contrary to us, and took it out of the way, nailing it to his cross; And having spoiled principalities and powers, he made a show of them openly, triumphing over them in it* (Colossians 2:13-15).

Joseph was faced with a difficult choice after discovering the woman he was to marry was pregnant, and yet he knew that taking Mary as his wife would be humiliating. Joseph chose to obey the angel's command which was to take her as his wife.

When we are confronted with difficulties in life, what would your plan be like? Would you reason from a social point or would it be from a spiritual point of view? The Bible gives ways of hindering things of that nature.

Let's look at a few spiritual qualities from a biblical point of view that may help in time of need. We want to look at these four qualities:
1.   <u>Righteousness</u>. Joseph, Mary's husband, was a just man, and not willing to make Mary his wife to be a public example. He was thinking to put her away privately (Matthew

1:19).

2. Discretion and Sensitivity. Joseph was showing in this verse. *Joseph being responsiveness to God: then he being raised from sleep did as the angel of the Lord had bidden him* (Matthew 1 :24).

3. Self-discipline. *And knew her not till she had brought forth her first-born son* (Matthew 1:25).

OLD TESTAMENT FAMILY (Genesis 18:12; Hosea 2:16)

Father Commanded A High Position: In the Old Testament, the father commanded a high position in the Hebrew family. Translated into English as husband means "lord," "master," "owner," or "possessor" (Genesis 18:12; Hosea 2:16). Because of his position, shared to some degree with his wife, a man expected to be treated as royalty by the rest of his family.

When we look at the respect Jesus gave His Father, we should understand what it means to be respectful to the family. God sent His only Son into the world to die for the sins of the people. Jesus could have done otherwise, but instead, He said, *Not my will, but your will be done* (Luke 22:42).

Jesus treated His father with royalty and His father respected Him for that. Jesus obeyed His father unto death when he said, *Not my will but your will be done.*

Jesus said behold, **the hour come yet, is now come, that you be scattered, every man to his own, and shall leave me alone: and yet I am not alone, because the Father is with me** (John 16:32). Let us be as Jesus was to His Father. A man expected to be treated with royalty by the rest of the family.

The fifth commandment carries this idea of the importance of the parents one step further when it states, *Honor your father and your mother* (Exodus 20:12). The word honor often times refers to one's response to God just as Jesus did. In other words, this commandment suggests that the parents should receive recognition similar to that given to God.

Confirming the Promise Made to Abraham: The heavenly guests being sent to confirm the promise lately made to Abraham, that he would have a son by Sarah, while they are receiving Abraham's kind entertainment, they returned his kindness. He receives angels, and has angel's rewards, a gracious message from heaven (Matthew 10:41).

Sarah Laughed Within Herself

Sarah Must Conceive by Faith: By faith, God will do what He has promised or will promise to them who keep His word by faith. This is just one of the illustrations showing us today that God loves us just as He loved the people of old. We can truly say the reason for the birth of Christ is not for the sake of just sending Him into the world because of those who are walking in darkness, rather it is because God loved us so much that He didn't want us to continue in darkness. He wants to redeem that which is His.

God sent his only Son into the world to reconcile us back to himself. We never think of the real reason why God sent His Son into the world. It is true we read the Scriptures concerning Him but do we truly understand? In reconciliation was taken by God while we were yet in sin and "enemies," to God, Christ died for us so that we wouldn't continue in sin (Roman 5:8, 10; Colossians 1:21).

In reading the Bible we understand reconciliation is God's own completed act, something that takes place before human action, such as confession, repentance, and restitution. God himself *has reconciled us to himself through Jesus Christ* (Corinthians 5:18). It is regarded in the gospels as *the word of reconciliation* (2-Corinthians 5: 19). And knowing *the terror of the Lord,"* which is intense fear, ethically speaking, the gospels implored, and persuaded men: *be reconciled to God* (2-Corinthians 5:20). Reconciliation is the process by which God and man are brought together again.

The Bible teaches that God and man are alienated from one another because of God's holiness and man's sinfulness. Although God loves the sinner (Roman 5:8), just because God loves the sinner isn't saying that He won't judge him for the sin. It is impossible for God not to judge sin (Hebrews 10:27).

In biblical reconciliation, both parties are affected. Through the sacrifice of Christ, man's sin is atoned and God's wrath is appeased. Now there is a relationship of hostility and alienation is changed into one of peace and fellowship. THIS IS WHAT THE BIRTH OF JESUS IS ALL ABOUT.

Sarah Should be Within Hearing (Hebrews 11:11)

Yet, Out of Sight: During Sarah and Abraham's time the women did not sit and eat with men, at least not with strangers, but were confined to themselves to their own apartments. Sarah was out of sight: but she must not have been out of hearing.

The Angels Knew Abraham: The angels enquired, "Where is your wife Sarah?" By naming her, they gave intimation enough to Abraham that, they seemed strangers to him, yet they very well knew Abraham's family. By enquiring after her, they showed a friendly kind concern for the family and relations of one whom they found respectful to them.

This Goes Back to Showing Principles of Respect for the Family: Showing respect for the family was what the angels showed in regards to Abraham when they inquired of Sarah to her husband Abraham, "Where is Sarah your wife?" Abraham said, "In the tent." It is most likely she received comfort from God and his promise that are in their place and in the way of their duty (Luke 2:8). So the promise is then renewed that she should have a son (Genesis 18:10).

A Gracious Message From Heaven: *He who receives a prophet in the name of a prophet receives a prophet's reward* (Matthew 10:41).

Received by Faith the Promise Made to Her: *Through faith also Sarah herself received strength to conceive seed* (Hebrews 11:11).

She Must Not be out of Hearing: *And they said unto him, where is Sarah your wife? And he said behold, in the tent* (Genesis 18:9).

MAN   WENT   CONTRARY   TO   GOD'S   WILL   (CONTINUED)

Value Life as God Does

Elements Making up our Bodies: The body is a lifeless shell until God brings it alive with His "breath of life. "When God removes His life-giving breath, our bodies once again return to dust. Therefore our life and worth come from God's Spirit. Many boast of their own strengths or achievements and the abilities as though they were the creator of everything of life.

Some feel worthless because of their abilities to not stand out; in reality, our worth comes not from our achievements but from the God of the universe, who chooses to give us the mysterious and miraculous gift of life. So I say to you, value life, as God does.

The Lord God formed man of the dust (Genesis 2:7-9).

By eating the fruit from the tree of life, Adam and Eve would have had eternal life (Genesis 2:16-17).

Embarrassment (Genesis 3:7-8).

Because Adam hearkened unto the voice of his wife (Genesis 3:17).

The Lord said my Spirit shall not always strive with man (Genesis 6:3).

The Lord God saw that the wickedness of men was great in the earth; And that every imagination of the thoughts of his heart was only evil continually (Genesis 6:5).

And it repented the Lord God that he had made on the earth, and it grieved him to his heart (Genesis 6:6-7).

And the earth also was corrupt before God, and the earth was filled with violence (Genesis 6:11).

Now lest he put forth his hand, and take also the tree of life and eat (Genesis 3 :22).

Therefore the Lord God sent him forth from the Garden of Eden (Genesis 3:23); (Ephesians 5:14-

18); (Ephesians 4:30); (Revelation 2:7).

Strengthening the Faith

Therefore Sarah laughed within herself, saying, After I am waxed old shall I have pleasure? My lord being old also.

<u>The Promises of the Messiah</u>: The promises of the Messiah are being repeated again. The Messiah was often repeated in the Old Testament, for the strengthening of the faith of God's people who believed. We are slow of heart to believe, and have need of line upon line to the same purport.

<u>Line Upon Line</u>: *Whom shall he teach knowledge? And whom shall he make to understand doctrine them who are weaned from the milk, and drawn from the breasts* (Jeremiah 6:10).

For precept must be upon precept, precept upon precept; Line, upon line, line upon line; here a little and there a little (Isaiah 28:9-10).

<u>The Word of Promise</u>: So here again, we are slow of heart to believe, and have need of line upon line to the same. This is that same word of promise which the apostle quotes in Romans and in Peter.

For this is the word of promise, at this time wills I come, and Sarah shall have a son (Roman 9:9).

Being born again, not of corruptible seed, but of incorruptible, by the word of God, which live and abide forever (1-Peter 1:23).

As that by the virtue of which Isaac was born; the same blessings which others have from the promise, which makes them very sweet and very sure; The spiritual seed of Abraham owe their life, and joy, and hope, and all to the promise.

Doubting and Mistrust

1. <u>Sarah's Laughter and Doubting</u>: Sarah thinks it is too good to be true, being too old to have a child, and therefore cannot find it in her heart to believe, so, she laughed to herself. It was not a pleasing laughter of faith you would think according to Genesis 18:12. Not like that of Abraham, but it was laughter of doubting and mistrust.

2. <u>Abraham Fell on His Face and Laughed</u>: (Genesis 17:7).

   <u>Sarah Laughed Within Herself</u>: (Genesis 18:12).

3. <u>References to Self</u>:

Nevertheless let everyone of you in particular so love his wife even as himself; and the wife see that she reverence her husband (Ephesians 5 :33).

Through faith also Sara herself received strength to conceive seed, and was delivered of a child when she was past age, because she judged him faithful who had promised (Hebrews **11:11**).

4.   <u>Sarah Obeyed Abraham</u>: Even as Sarah obeyed Abraham, calling him lord: whose daughters you are, as long as you do the will of your lord, and are not afraid with any amazement (l-Peter 3:6).

The same thing may be done from very different principles, of which God only, who knows the heart, can judge. The great objection which Sarah could not get over was her age: ("I am waxed old), and past childbearing in the course of nature, especially having been hitherto barren, and (which magnifies the difficulty) my lord is (old also)," Sarah calls Abraham her lord is old also.

Imitation of All Christians

<u>Imitation</u>: The imitation is shown in 1-Peter which is for reference of Christians today to go by. just as it was for the old day, it was the only good word in this saying of Sarah, saying, and the Holy Ghost takes notice of it to her honor, and recommends it to the imitation of all Christian wives. The only reason I am writing and putting the words in the way I am is because of looking as well as thinking with a spiritual mind. Thinking and looking at it in any other way will not lead the reader to read with a spiritual-like manner, in token of respect and subjection.

The angel reproves the expressions of Sarah's distrust, though Sarah was most kindly and generously entertaining the angels. Yet when she did amiss, they reproved her for it, as Christ reproved Martha in her own house. If our friends be kind to us, we must not therefore be so unkind to them as to suffer sin upon them.

1.   <u>The Angel Reproves the Expressions of Sarah's Distrust</u>: *And the Lord said unto Abraham, wherefore did Sarah laugh, saying, Shall I of a surety bear a child even though I am old? Is anything too hard for the Lord? At the time of life I will return unto you, according to the time of life, and Sarah shall have a son* (Genesis 18:13- 14).

2.   <u>Christ Reproved Martha in her House</u>: *But Martha was much encumbered about serving, and came to him, and said, Lord, do you not care that my sister has left me to serve alone? Bid her therefore that she help me. And Jesus answered and said unto her,* ***Martha, Martha, you are careful and troubled about many things*** (Luke 10:40-41).

3.   <u>Zachariah's Wife was Old</u>: *And Zacharias said unto the angel, whereby shall I know this?*

87

For I am an old man, and my wife well stricken in years (Luke 1: 18).

Laughter of a Fool is Vanity

<u>The Laughter of a Fool is Vanity</u>: When we laugh, it is good to enquire into the reason for our laughter. It should not be the laughter of the fool (Ecclesiastes 7:6). Our unbelief and distrust is a great offence to the God of heaven. He justly takes it ill to have the objections of sense set up in contradiction to His promise (Luke 1:18).

Question: Which is enough to answer all the cavils of flesh is and blood (is anything too hard for God?)

- Is anything so secret as to escape his cognizance? (No) not Sarah's laughing, though it was only within herself.

- Is anything so difficult as to exceed his power? (No) not the giving of a child to Sarah in her old age.

Sarah foolishly endeavors to conceal her fault. She denied, saying, "I did not laugh

4.   *Then Sarah denied, saying, I laughed not, for she was afraid. And she said, Nay, but you did laugh* (Genesis 18: 15).

There seems to be in Sarah's heart a retraction of her distrust. Now Sarah perceived, by laying circumstances together, that it was a divine promise which had been made concerning her. She then renounced all doubting distrustful thoughts about it. Sarah withal a sinful attempt to cover a sin with a lie. It's a shame to do amiss, but a greater shame to deny it; thereby we add iniquity to our iniquity.

We deceive ourselves if we think to impose upon God. He can and will bring truth to light, as to our shame. He who covers their sin cannot prosper, for the day is coming which will discover it.

5.   <u>Betrays in a Snare</u>: *And of whom have you been afraid or feared, that you have lied, and have not remembered me, nor laid it to your heart? Have not I held my peace even of old and you fairest me not* (Isaiah 57:11).

THE BEST CHRISTMAS EVER

The best Christmas you could ever have is to have someone to love you in spite of rather than because of; when you love someone because of, usually it involves emotions. When emotions are involved it brings us to the attention of something being done because of a deed rather than in spite of.

When we think of the reason for Christmas we can't help but look back into the old days during the time of creation when God looked and saw that the wickedness of man was great and the imagination of the thoughts of his heart was only evil continually (Genesis 6:5, 6). *And it repented the Lord that he had made man on the earth, and it grieved him at his heart.*

God created Adam in his image and likeness, He made man for his purse which was to serve and worship Him, having dominion over His creation (Genesis 1:26). *We are asked to not grieve the Holy Spirit of God whereby we are sealed until the day of redemption* (Ephesians 4:30).

This brings us around to what Christmas is all about. God so loved the world that He gave his only Son to get back that which is His. The entire gospel comes to a focus in this one saying. God's love is not static or self-centered; it reaches out into the world to every man woman boy and girl, to draw them in; and to give them a new life in him (John 3:16).

In Christ Jesus we can have a new life, just as we have a new year to look forward to. This also can give a new beginning knowing that we can do all thing through Christ Jesus who strength us. May the heavens ever smile upon you and the blessings of the highest are with you. This year and the years to come, just stay in His will and He will make things well with you. He promises to give you your heart's desires only if you delight yourself in Him and trust Him and He shall bring it to pass. That's a promise He made to them who love, trust, and have faith in His word, (Psalm 37:4-7). (Genesis 6:5-6; John 3:16) is the reason for the season. God sent His Son into the world to save them who trust by faith in believing.

WORKSHEET: Noah's Family (Genesis 6-8

Inquire to the Reasons

TOPICS: Covenant, Creation, Death, Earth, Evil, God, Judgment, Life, Life-style, Punishment, Rebellion, Sacrifice, Salvation, Sin, Society, World, and Worship;

In these topics are questions on why God did the things He did. Out of these questions there will be true or false questions based on Scripture from GENESIS 6, 7, and 8.

OPEN IT:
1.   What is the most significant natural disaster you have witnessed or experienced?
2.   What do you find most disturbing about society today?

EXPLORE IT:
1.   Why did God limit man's life span to a hundred and twenty years? (Genesis 6: 1-3)
2.   What are the main events in these verses? (Genesis 6:1-8:22)
3.   Why did God say He would wipe mankind off the face of the earth? (Genesis 6:5-7)
4.   What kind of man was Noah? (Genesis 6:8-10)
5.   What did God tell Noah to build and why (Genesis 6: 11-14)
6.   What did God tell Noah He was going to destroy? (Genesis 6: 17)
7.   What did God say He would establish with Noah? (Genesis 6:18)
8.   With what did God instruct Noah to fill the ark with? (Genesis 6:19-21)
9.   Why did God tell Noah he was allowed to enter the ark? (Genesis 7: 1)
10.   What happened to all the living creatures that were not on the ark? (Genesis 7 :21-23)
11.   What happened after the flood ended but before Noah and his family got off the ark? (Genesis 8:1-14)
12.   Why did God tell Noah to bring the animals off the ark? (Genesis 8:15-17)
13.   What did Noah do when he got off the ark? (Genesis 8:20)
14.   How did the Lord respond to Noah's offering? (Genesis 8:21-22)

WORKSHEET: GENESIS 6-8 (continued)

UNDERLINE THE ANSWER

1.   Why did God (limit life to a hundred and twenty years)?
And it came to pass, when men began to multiply on the face of the earth, and daughters were born unto them, that the sons of God saw the daughters of men that they were fair; and they took them wives of all which they chose.
And the Lord said, My spirit shall not always strive with man, for that he also is flesh: yet his days shall be an hundred and twenty years (Genesis 6:1-3).

2.   What are the (events) in these verses?
And it came to pass, when men began to multiply on the face of the earth, and daughters were born unto them (Genesis 6: 1).
While the earth remain, seed time and harvest, and cold and heat, and summer and winter, and day and night shall not cease (Genesis 8:22).

3.   What kind of man was Noah?
But Noah found grace in the eyes of the Lord. These are the generations of Noah: Noah was a just man and perfect in his generation, and Noah walked with God. And Noah begat three sons, (Shem, Ham, and Japheth) (Genesis 6:8-10).

4.   What did God tell Noah to build and why?
The earth also was corrupt before God, and the earth was filled with violence. And God looked upon the earth, and, behold, it was corrupt; for all flesh had corrupted his way upon the earth. And God said unto Noah, the end of all flesh is come before me: for the earth is filled with violence through them, and behold, I will destroy them with the earth. Make you an ark of gopher wood; rooms shall you make in the ark, and shall pitch it within and without with pitch (Genesis 6: 11-14).

5.   What did God tell Noah He was going to destroy?
And, behold, I, do bring a flood of waters upon the earth, to destroy all flesh, wherein is the breath of life, from under heaven; and everything that is in the earth shall die (Genesis 6:17).

6.   What did God say He would establish with Noah?
But with you will I establish my covenant; and you shall come into the ark, you and your sons, and their wives with you.

7.   With what did God instruct Noah to fill the ark with?
And of every living thing of all flesh, two of every sort shall you bring into the ark, to keep them alive with you; they shall be male and female. Of fowls after their kind, and of cattle after their kind, of every creeping thing of the earth after his kind, two of every sort shall come unto you, to keep them alive. And take you unto you of all food that is eaten, and you shall gather it to you, and it shall be for food for you, and for them (Genesis 6:19-21).

8.   Why did God tell Noah he was allowed to enter the ark?

And the Lord said unto Noah, come you and your house into the ark, for you have I seen righteous before me in this generation (Genesis 7:1).

9.   What happened to all the living creatures that were not on the ark?

And all flesh died that moved upon the earth, both of fowl, and of cattle, and of beast, and thing that creep upon the earth, and every man: all in whose nostrils was the breath of life, of all that was in the dry land, died. And every living substance was destroyed which was upon the face of the ground, both man, and cattle, and the creeping things, and the fowl of the heaven; and they were destroyed from the earth: and Noah only remained alive, and they that were with him in the ark (Genesis 7:21-23).

10.   What happened after the flood ended but before Noah and his family got off the ark?

And God remembered Noah, and every living thing, and all the cattle that was with him in the ark: and God made a wind to pass over the earth, and the ware assuaged; the fountains also of the deep and the windows of heaven were stopped, and the rain from heaven was restrained.

11.   What happened to Noah and his family after the flood?

And the water returned from off the earth continually: and after the end of the hundred and fifty days the waters were abated. And the ark rested in the seventh month, on the seventeenth day of the month, upon the mountains of Ararat. And the water decreased continually until the tenth month: in the tenth month, on the first day of the month, were the top of the mountains seen. And it came to pass at the end of forty days, that Noah opened the window of the ark which he had made: And he sent forth a raven, which went forth to and fro, until the waters were dried up from off the earth. Also he sent forth a dove from him, to see if the Water were abated from off the face of the ground; But the dove found no rest for the sole of her feet, and she returned unto him into the ark, for the waters were on the face of the whole earth: then he put forth his hand, and took her, and pulled her in unto him into the ark. And he stayed yet other seven days; and again he sent forth the dove out of the ark; and the dove came in to him in the evening; and , Lo, in her moth was an olive leaf plucked off: so Noah knew that the waters were abated from off the earth (Genesis 8:3-14).

And he stayed yet other seven days; and sent forth the dove; which returned not again unto him anymore. And it came to pass in the six hundredth and first year, in the first month, the first day of the month, the waters were dried up from off the earth: and Noah removed the covering of the ark, and looked, and behold, the face of the ground was dry. And in the second month, on the seven and twentieth day of the month, was the earth dried. This concludes verses one through fourteen of (Genesis 8:12-14).

12.   Why did God tell Noah to bring the animals into the ark?

And God spoke unto Noah, saying, go forth of the ark, you, and your wife, and your sons, and their son's wives with you. Bring forth with you every living thing that is with you, of all flesh, both of fowl, and of cattle, and of every creeping thing upon the earth; that they may breed abundantly in the earth, and be fruitful, and multiply upon the earth (Genesis 8:15-17).

13.   What did Noah do when he got off the ark?

And Noah built an altar unto the Lord; and took of every clean beast, and of every clean fowl, and offered burnt offerings on the altar (Genesis 8:20)

14.   How did the Lord respond to Noah's offering?

And the Lord smelled a sweet savor and the Lord said in his heart, I will not again curse the ground any more for man's sake; for the imagination of man's heart is evil from his youth; neither will I again smite any more everything living, as I have done. While the earth remain, seed time and harvest, and cold and heat, and summer and winter, and day and night shall not cease (Genesis 8:21-22).

THIS IS A REFLECTIION OF WHAT YOU HAVE READ:

You are to answer these questions based upon what you have learned from reading Genesis 6, 7 and 8

1.   How does Noah's world compare to our society?

2.   Why was God willing to destroy most every living thing?

3.   Who is someone you know who you would describe as blameless?

4.   How can we maintain a blameless reputation?

5.   What is the significance of God's covenant with Noah?

6.   How does God respond to the evil in our society?

7.   why did Noah worship God after getting off the ark?

8.   Why do you think God promised never to destroy the earth with a flood again?

9.   Among whom do you have a reputation for serving God?

10.   What is one thing you can do to cultivate a blameless reputation among your coworkers or your neighbors?

11.   What is one act of protection or provision from God for which you want to praise Him?

SOLOMON DISOBEYED GOD

Solomon Went Contrary to the Will of God

The Bible describes the condition with regard to the circumstances in which a man must be married. Solomon went contrary to the will of God and married an unbeliever. Solomon is a prime example in showing disobeying God's commandment and married 700 wives.

And he had seven hundred wives, princesses, and Three hundred concubines: and his wises turned Away his heart 1-King 11:3).

The tragedy of the final years of his life is summarized in one sentence: *For it came to pass, when Solomon was old, that his wives turned away his heart after other gods: and his heart was not perfect with the Lord his God, as was the heart of David his father* (1-King 11:4).

His wives and their gods caused Solomon to take his eyes off the living God:

TOPICS:
Age, Anger, Appearance, Attitude, Children, Covenant, Death, Devotion, Enemies, Evil, Gifts, Heart, History, Idolatry, Law, Marriage, Murder, Prophecy, Punishment, Rebellion, Rewards, Righteousness, Running, Sacrifice, Wives;

WHAT EXPERIENCE DO YOU HAVE?
1.   Do you have any experiences of yourself or someone close to you "getting in with the wrong crowd"?
2.   What are the potential problems of a marriage between two people of different faith?
3.   What was one of Solomon's primary downfall and areas of disobedience against God? (1-King 11:3).
4.   How many wives did Solomon marry? (l-King 11:3).
5.   What happened to Solomon's devotion to God as he got older? (l-King 11:4)?
6.   What gods did Solomon allow to be worshiped in Israel because of his foreign wives? 1-11:5-8).

God's Ideal for the Family

What's Instilled in the Believers of God? God's ideal for the family is that it be a harmonious unit where love for God and neighbor are instilled into each member. If the couple is divided, especially over religious beliefs, they can never have the harmony and sense of common purpose that God desires. Therefore, Old Testament believers were instructed not to marry foreigners who would hinder their faith and bring strife to the marriage. Likewise the Bible commanded the New Testament believers, "do not be unequally yoked together with unbelievers."

1.   <u>Harmonious Unit Instilled into Each Member</u>: *And these words, which I command you this day, shall be in your heart: And you shall teach them diligently unto your children, and shall talk of them when you Sit test in your homes, and when you walk by the way, and when you lie down, and when you rise up. And you shall bind them for a sign upon your hand, and they shall be as frontlets between your eyes. And you shall write them upon the posts of your house, and on your gates* (Deuteronomy 6:6-9).

2.   <u>God Instructed Not to Marry Foreigners</u>: *But you shall destroy their altars, break their images, and cut Down their groves: For you shall worship no other god: for the Lord, whose name is Jealous, is a jealous God: Lest you make a covenant with the inhabitants of the land, and they go a whoring after their gods, and do sacrifice unto their gods, and one call you, and you eat of his sacrifice; and you take of their daughters unto your sons, and their daughters go a whoring after their gods, and make your sons go a whoring after their gods* (Exodus 34:13-16).

3.   <u>Not To Marry Foreigner Who Would Bring Strife or Hinder Faith</u>: *Neither shall you make marriages with them; your daughter you shall not give to your sons or you daughter shall you take unto your sons. For they will turn away your son from following me that they may serve other gods: so will the anger of the Lord be kindled against you, and destroy you suddenly* (Deuteronomy 7:3-4).

Origin of Marriage

<u>Marriage was Instituted by God</u>: Biblical teaching or commanded in the New Testament believers, "Do not be unequally yoked together with unbelievers."
After God created Adam, he declared, "It is not good that man should be alone. "
Then he created woman and united the couple; and they became "one flesh" thus the family was designed by God to provide companionship for the various members of the family. In addition, the institution of marriage was approved and sanctioned by the Lord.

1.   *Do not be unequally yoked* (2-Corinthians 6:14).

2.   *Man should not be alone* (Genesis 2:18).
3.   *And the Lord God caused a deep sleep upon Adam and took one of his ribs and made a companion* (Genesis 2:21).

This union of a man and a woman as husband and wife, which becomes the foundation for a home and family. So, again, marriage was instituted by God when he collected, *It is not good that man should be alone; I will make him a helper which is to be a companion to him.*

This is now bone of my bones and flesh of my flesh; she shall be called woman, because she was taken out of man (Genesis 2:23). This passage also emphasizes the truth that *a man shall leave his father and mother and be joined to his wife, and they shall become one flesh* (Genesis 2:24). This suggests that God's ideal is for a man to be the husband of one wife and for the marriage to be permanent.

WORKSHEET: Sexual Immorality

TOPICS:

Adultery, Body, Desires, Spirit, Immorality, Lust, Marriage, Maturity, Morality, Sex, Sin, Singleness, Slavery, Temptation, Weaknesses

OPEN IT:

1.	In what ways do Americans typically mistreat their bodies?
2.	In your opinion, what are the biggest challenges to sexual purity in our society?

EXPLORE IT:

3.	What did the writer mean by saying, "I will not be mastered by anything"? (1-Corinthians 6:12)
4.	Why should we abstain from sex outside of marriage? (l-Corinthians 6:12-20)
5.	What value does God place on our bodies? (l-Corinthians 6:12-20)
6.	What will God destroy? And why 1-Corinthians 6:13)
7.	For what are our bodies meant? (1-Corinthians 6:13)
8.	What promise is given to Christians because God raised Jesus from the dead? (1-Corinthians 6:14)
9.	What makes our bodies special? (1-Corinthians 6:15)
10.	What's wrong with sex outside of marriage? (1-Corinthians 6:15-16)
11.	Why is it not possible to be one with both Christ and a prostitute? (Corinthians 6:15-17)
12.	What does it mean to be one with Christ in spirit? (l-Corinthians 6: 17)
13.	How is sexual immorality different from other sins? 1-Corinthians 6:18)
14.	How are Christians' bodies unique? 1-Corinthians 6:19-20).

GET IT:

15.	How can we distinguish between what is merely permissible and what is beneficial?
16.	How should we treat our bodies if they are actually temples of the Holy Spirit?
17.	How do advertising and other media encourage wrong attitudes about our bodies?
18. How do friends, coworkers, and other peers encourage wrong attitudes about our bodies?
19.	How does sexually uniting with someone outside of marriage affect a person?
20.	In what specific ways is it possible for you to honor God with your body?
12.	What can a person do to master natural human desires that can lead to sin?
22.	What can you do to master areas of your life that could cause you to sin against your body?
23.	How can we avoid compromises that lead to sexual sin?

APPLY IT:

24.	In what way can you remind yourself this week that you were bought at a price and are God's temple?

25.   In what settings or situations should you take precaution against sexual immorality? Read 1-Corinthians 6:12-20) You will be able to answer these questions, let us begin reading;

<u>1-CORINTHIANS 6:12-20</u>:

[12]   *All things are lawful unto me, but all things are not expedient: all things are lawful for me, but I will not be brought under the power of any.*

[13]   *Meats for the belly, and the belly for meats: but God shall destroy both it and them. Now the body is not for fornication, but for the Lord, and the Lord for the body.*

[14]   *And God has both raise up the Lord, and will also rise up us by his own power.*

[15]   *Know you not that your bodies are the members of Christ? Shall I then take the members of Christ, and make them the members of a harlot? God forbid.*

[16]   *What? Know you not that he which is joined to a harlot is one body? For two, said he, shall be one flesh.*

[17]   *But he who is joined unto the Lord is one spirit.*

[18]   *Flee fornication every sin that a man do is without the body; but he who committed fornication sonnet against his own body .*

[19]   *What? Know you not that your body is the temple of the Holy Ghost which is in you, which you have of God, and you are not of your own?*

[20]   *For you are bought with a price: therefore glorify God in your body, and in your spirit, which are God's.*

In reading with a spiritual mind you should be able to answer the questions in (why and how). Remember that you were bought at a price and you are God's body. Reflect on what settings or situations should you take precautions against sexual immorality.

WORKSHEET: God's Desire for His People

<u>MARRY WITHIN THE BODY OF BELIEVERS</u>: The Mosaic Law clearly stated that an Israelite was never you marry a Canaanite. The Israelite would be constantly tempted to embrace the spouse's god as well;

<u>I WILL MAKE A COVENANT</u> (Exodus 34:10-17):

[10]   And he said, Behold, I will make a covenant before all your people I will do marvels, such as have not been done in all the earth, nor in any nation: and all the people among you shall see the work of the Lord: for it is a terrible thing that I will do with you

[11]   Observe you that which I command you this day: behold, I drive out before you the (Arnorite), and the (Canaanite), and the (Hittite), and the (Perizzite), and the (Hivite), and the (Jebusite).

[12]   Take heed to thyself, lest you make a covenant with the inhabotants of the land whither you go, lest it be for a snare in the midst of you

[13]   But you shall destroy their altars, break their images, and cut down their groves:

[14]   For you shall worship no other god: for the Lord, whose name is Jealous, is a jealous God:

[15[Lest you make a covenant with the inhabitants of the land, and they go a whoring after their gods, and do sacrifice unto their gods, and one call you, and you eat of his sacrifice;

[16]   And you take of their (daughters) unto your (sons), and their (daughters) go a whoring after their (gods), and make your (sons go a whoring after their gods)

[17] You shall make no (molten gods).

<u>TOPICS</u>:
Compassion, Covenant, Jealousy, Obedience, Worship,

<u>OPEN IT AND EXPLORE IT</u>:
1.   What is the most dangerous situation you have ever been in?
2.   Who is someone who helped you during one of your biggest blunders?
3.   When you're finishing an important project, what distracts you most?
4.   What did God ask Moses to do after the first set of stone tablets broke? (Exodus 34:1)
5.   What directions did God give Moses about coming to Mount Sinai (Exodus 34:2,3)
6.   What did the Lord do when Moses followed His instructions? (Exodus 34:4-5)
7.   How did God proclaim to Moses who He was? (Exodus 34:6-7)
8.   What was Moses' response to God's proclamation? (Exodus 34:8, 9)
9.   What did God say He would do for the Israelites? (Exodus 34: 10,11)
10.   -What did God say to the Israelites about making treaties? (Exodus 34:12)
11.   Why were the Israelites not to worship other gods? (Exodus 34:13-14)
12.   What did God tell Moses about foreign idols? (Exodus 34: 15-17)
13.   In what way was Moses told to celebrate the feasts? (Exodus 34:18-23)
14.   What was the blessing associated with celebrating the feast? (Exodus 34:24)

15.   What other instructions did God give Moses concerning the offerings? (Exodus 34:25-26)

16.   What were the words of the covenant called? (Exodus 34:27-28)

17.   What was Moses not aware of when he came down from the mountain (Exodus 34:29)

18.   Who was afraid of Moses? (Exodus 34:30-31)

19.   What happened after Moses finished speaking to all the Israelites? (Exodus 34:32-35)

GET IT:

20.   How do you feel when you talk to God about the same problem over and over?

21.   What doesn't God even tire of our repentance and dependence on Him for forgiveness? Does God become weary of our repentance? (Jeremiah 15:6)

22.   How would you have felt if you were Moses when returning for a second set of tablets?

23.   How are people reluctant to ask for forgiveness?

24.   How do people in our society show compassion?

25.   What makes people stand in awe of heroic believers such as mother Teresa?

26.   What was it about Moses' radiance that made people afraid of him?

27.   How does it make you feel knowing that God is jealous for you?

28.   In what way can a Christian reflect God's glory to others?

APPLY IT:

29.   With what prayer could you accept God's compassion and love for you?

30.   How can you demonstrate the grace of God in your life?

31.   In what area of life can you make your life reflect God to others?

Read Exodus 34:1-35 and underline each of the questions you are asked in the topics

EXPLORE IT:
Read Exodus 34:1-35 and underline each of the questions you are asked in the topics

1.   WHAT DID GOD ASK MOSES TO DO?

And the Lord said unto Moses, hew the two tables of stone like unto the first: and I will write upon these tables the words that were in the first tables, which you broke (Exodus 34:1).

2.   WHAT DIRECTION DID GOD GIVE MOSES?

And be ready in the morning, and come up in the morning unto Mount Sinai, and present yourself there to me in the top of the mount. And no man shall come up with you, neither let any man be seen throughout all the mount, neither let the flocks nor herds feed before the mount (Exodus 34:2-3).

3.   WHAT DID THE LORD DO WHEN MOSES FOLLOWED HIS INSTRUCTIONS?

And he hewed two tables of stone like unto the first, and Moses rose up early in the morning, and went up unto mount Sinai, as the Lord had commanded him, and took in his hand the two tables of stone. And the Lord descended in the cloud, and stood with him there, and proclaimed the name of the Lord (EXODUS 34:4-5).

4.   HOW DID GOD PROCLAIM TO MOSES WHO HE WAS?

And the Lord passed by before him, and proclaimed, the Lord, the Lord God, merciful and gracious, longsuffering, and abundant in goodness and true, Keeping mercy for thousands, forgiving iniquity and transgression and sin, and that will by no means clear the guilty; visiting the iniquity of the fathers upon the children, and upon the children's children, unto the third and to the fourth generation (Exodus 34:6-7).

5.   WHAT WAS MOSES' RESPONSE TO GOD'S PROCLAMATION?

And Moses made haste, and bowed his head toward the earth, and worshiped. And he said, If now I have found grace in your sight, 0 Lord, let my Lord, I pray thee, go among us, for it is a stiff-necked people; and pardon our iniquity and our sin, and take us for your inheritance (Exodus 34:8-9).

6.   WHAT DID GOD SAY HE WOULD DO FOR THE ISRAELITES?

And he said, behold, I make a covenant: before all your people I will do marvels, such as have not been done in all the earth, nor in any nation: and all the people among which you are shall see the work of the Lord: for it is a terrible thing that I will do with you. Observe you that which I command you this day: behold, I drive out before you the Amorite, and the Canaanite, and the Jebusite (Exodus 34:10-11).

7.   WHAT DID GOD SAY TO THE ISRAELITES?

Take heed to your-self, lest you make a covenant with the inhabitants of the land where you go, lest it be for a snare in the midst of you (Exodus 34: 12).

8.   WHY WERE THE ISRAELITES NOT TO WORSHIP OTHER GODS?

But you shall destroy their altars, break their images, and cut down their groves: For you shall worship no other god: for the Lord, whose name is Jealous, is a jealous God (Exodus 34:13-14).

9.   WHAT DID GOD TELL MOSES ABOUT FOREIGN IDOLS?

Lest you make a covenant with the inhabitants of the land, and they go a whoring after their gods, and do sacrifice unto their gods, and one call you, and you eat of his sacrifice; And you take of their daughters unto your sons, and their daughters go a whoring after their gods, and make your sons go a whoring after their gods. You shall make you no molten gods (Exodus 34:15-17).

10.   IN WHAT WAY WERE MOSES TOLD TO CELEBRATE THE FEASTS?

The feast of unleavened bread shall you keep. Seven days you shall eat unleavened bread, as I commanded you, in the time of the month Abib: for in the month Abib you came out from Egypt. All that open the matrix is mine; and every firstling among your cattle; whether ox or sheep, that is male. But the firstling of an ass you shall redeem with a lamb: and if you redeem him not, then shall you break his neck. All the firstborn of your sons you shall redeem. And none shall appear before me empty. Six days you shall work, but on the (seventh) day you shall (rest). And you shall observe the feast of weeks, of the first-fruits of wheat harvest, and the feast of ingathering at the year's end. Thrice in the year shall all your men children appear before the Lord God, the God of Israel (Exodus 34: 18-23).

11.   WHA T WAS THE BLESSING ASSOCIATED WITH CELEBRATING THE FEASTS?

For I will cast out the nations before you, and enlarge your borders: neither shall any man desire your land, when you shall go up to appear before the Lord your God thrice in the year (Exodus 34:24).

12.   WHAT OTHER INSTRUCTIONS DID GOD GIVE MOSES CONCERNING OFFERINGS?

You shall not offer the blood of my sacrifice with leaven; neither shall the sacrifice of the fest of the Passover be left unto the morning. The first of the first-fruits of your land you shall bring unto the house of the Lord your God (Exodus 34:25-26).

13.   WHAT WERE THE WORDS OF THE COVENANT CALLED?

And the Lord said unto Moses, write these words: for after the tenor of these words I have made a covenant with you and with Israel. And he was there with the Lord forty days and forty nights; he did neither eat bread, nor drink water. And he wrote upon the tables the words of the covenant, the Ten Commandment (Exodus 34:27-28).

14.   WHAT WAS MOSES NOT A WARE OF WHEN HE CAME DOWN THE MOUNTAIN?

And it came to pass, when Moses came down from mount Sinai with the two tables of testimony in Moses' hand, when he came down from the mount, that Moses wits not that the skin of his face shone while he talked with them (Exodus 34:29).

15.   WHO WAS AFRAID OF MOSES?

And when Aaron and all the children of Israel saw Moses, behold, the skin of his face shone; and they were afraid to come nigh him. And Moses called unto them, and Aaron and all the rulers of the congregation returned unto him: and Moses talked with them (Exodus 34:30-31).

16.   WHA T HAPPENED AFTER MOSES FINISHED SPEAKING TO ALL THE ISRAELITES?

And afterward all the children of Israel came nigh: and he gave them in commandment all that the Lord had spoken with him in Mount Sinai. And till Moses had done speaking with them, he put a vial on his face. But when Moses went in before the Lord to speak with him, he took the vial off, until he came out. And he came out, and space unto the children of Israel that which he was commanded. And the children of Israel saw the face of Moses that the skin of Moses' face shone: and Moses put the vial upon his face again, until he went in to speak with him (Exodus 34:32-35).

17.   HOW DO YOU FEEL WHEN YOU TALK TO GOD ABOUT THE SAME PROBLEM OVER AND OVER?

18.   WHY DOESN'T GOD EVER TIRE OF OUR REPENTANCE AND DENDENCE ON HIM FOR FORGIVENESS (JEREMIAH 15:6).(ACTS I7:30-32)

19.   HOW WOULD YOU HAVE FELT IF YOU WERE MOSES AFTER RETURNING FOR A SENCOND SET OF TABLETS?

20.   HOW ARE PEOPLE RELUCTANT TO ASK FORFORGIVENESS?

21.   HOW DO PEOPLE IN OUR SOCIETY SHOW COMPASSION?

22.   WHAT MAKES PEOPLE STAND IN A WE OF HEROIG BELIEVERS SUCH AS MOTHER TERESA?

23.   WHAT WAS IT ABOUT MOSES' RADIANCE THAT MADE PEOPLE AFRAID OF HIM?

24.   HOW DOES IT MAKE YOU FEEL KNOWING THAT GOD IS JEALOUS FOR YOU?

25.   IN WHAT WAY CAN A CHRISTIAN REFLECT GOD'S GLORY TO OTHER?
APPLY IT

26.   WITH WHAT PRA YER COULD YOU ACCEPT GOD'S COMPASSION AND LOVE FOR YOU?

27.   HOW CAN YOU DEMONSTRATE THE GRACE OF GOD IN YOUR LIFE?

28.   IN WHAT AREA OF LIFE CAN YOU MAKE YOUR LIFE REFLECT GOD TO OTHERS?

THIS CONCLUDES THE REFLECTIONS WORKSHEET OF GOD'S DESIRE FOR THIS PEOPLE

WORKSHEET: Marriages (Deuteronomy 7)

TOPICS:
Blessing, Change, Faithfulness, Holy, Power, Promises, Relation

In this reflection you will be asked to answer questions and give some thoughts concerning what you think based on the Scripture you have read, you will be ask to underline some of the questions, you must read the given Scriptures in order to give the right answer. You have the topics at the top of the page in which you can draw from.

This is still about the people of God concerning marriages being unequally yoked together with unbelievers." At this point what is being done is laying the foundation for the family of God, you must understand what the expectations of God for the family.

OPEN IT:
1.   What do you find most fascinating about ancient empires?

2.   What "gods" are worshiped din our culture today?

3.   How do some people worship things without even realizing it?

EXPLORE IT:
4.   What did God Command the Israelites to do when He drove out the Nation? (Deuteronomy 7:1-2)
5.   For what reason are the Israelites told not to intermarry? (Deuteronomy 7:3-4)
6.   What are the people told to do with the altars of idols? (Deuteronomy 7:6)
7.   How is Israel the treasured possession of God? (Deuteronomy 7:6)
8.   What was the motive of God to choose Israel over other nations? Deuteronomy 7:7-8)
9.   How faithful is God? (Deuteronomy 7:9-10)
10.   To what was Israel told to pay special attention? (Deuteronomy 7:11-l2)
11.   How would Israel be blessed by obeying God? (Deuteronomy 7:13-15)
12.   How would other gods hurt Israel's relationship with God? (Deuteronomy 7: I6)
13.   What fearful question do the people of Israel ask? (Deuteronomy 7:17)
14.   How was Israel told not to fear the other nation? (Deuteronomy 7:18-20)
15.   What characteristics of God are described in this passage? (Deuteronomy 7:21)
16.   How was Israel promised by God to drive out the other nation? (Deuteronomy 7:22-24)
17.   What was Israel told to do with the pagan gods? (Deuteronomy 7:25-26)

GET IT: Read the Deuteronomy 7 then answer the questions.
18.   What do you think others think of when they hear the word idol?
19.   What is the danger of Christians' following idols?

20. In what way do people sometimes make idols out of other people? 21-how do impersonal idols ruin a personal relationship with God?

22. What type of statement did God make by asking for the complete destruction of all idols?

23. How does the warning God gave Israel about idols relate to us today? 24-How id God able to drive out the idols in a person's life?

APPLY IT:
25-What is an idol you need to forsake in order to follow God faithfully? 26-How can you bolster your confidence in the great and awesome power of God?

SCRIPTURE:
Neither shall you make marriages with them; your daughter shall not give onto his son, nor his daughter shall you take unto your son For they will turn away your son from following me, that they may serve other gods: so will the anger of the Lord be kindled against you, and destroy you suddenly (Deuteronomy 7:3-4)

Driving Out the Nations (Deuteronomy 7)

If you are married and thinking about getting a divorce this will give you something to think about. If you aren't married maybe you will think a little harder before doing so. If your aren't a member of the household of God, it would be good if you would join up with the family of God. All you need is to have faith and to believe in His teachings which is the word given by Jesus Christ the Son of the living God. I am sure you believe in something, so why not believe and have faith where it will count for something eternally, otherwise, you are without hope and a promise which leads to no place of peace of mind.

DRIVING OUT THE NATION (DEUTERONOMY 7:1-26)

TOPICS:
Blessing, Change, Faithfulness, Holy, Power, Promises, Religion

OPEN IT:
1. What do you find most fascinating about ancient empires?
2. What "gods" are worshiped in our culture today?
3. How do some people worship things without even realizing it?

EXPLORE IT:
You will be given chapter and verses. Underline the questions that is asked.

4. WHAT DID GOD COMMAND THE ISRAELITES TO DO WHEN HE DROVE OUT THE NATIONS?
When the Lord your God shall bring you into the land where you are to go to possess it, and have cast

out many nations before you, the Hittites, and the Girgashites, and the Amorites, and the Canaanites, and the Perizzites, and the Hivites, and the Jebusites, seven nations greater and mightier than you; And when the Lord your God shall deliver them before you; you shall smite them, and utterly destroy them; you shall make no covenant with them, nor show mercy unto them (Deuteronomy 7:1-2).

5.   FOR WHAT REASON ARE THE ISRAELITES TOLD NOT TO INTERMARRY?

Neither shall you make marriage with them; your daughter you shall not give unto his son, nor his daughter shall you take unto your son. For they will turn away your son from following me, that they may serve other gods: so will the anger of the Lord be kindled against you, and destroy you suddenly (Deuteronomy 7:3-4).

WHAT THE PEOPLE WERE TOLD

6.   WHAT ARE THE PEOPLE TOLD TO DO WITH THE ALTARS OF IDLOS?

But this shall you deal with them; you shall destroy their altars, and break down their images, and cut down their groves, and bum their graven images with fire (Deuteronomy 7:5).

7.   HOW IS ISRAEL THE TREASURED POSSESSION OF GOD?

For you are a holy people unto the Lord your God: the Lord your God has chosen you to be a special people unto himself, above all people that are upon the face of the earth (Deuteronomy 7:6).

8.   WHAT WAS THE MOTIVE OF GOD TO CHOOSE ISRAEL OVER OTHER NATIONS?

The Lord did not set his love upon you, nor choose you, because you were more in numbers than any people; for you were the fewest of all people: But because the Lord loved you, and because he would keep the oath which he had sworn unto your fathers, hath the Lord brought you out with a mighty hand, and redeemed you out of the house of Egypt (Deuteronomy 7:7-8).

9.   HOW FAITHFUL IS GOD?

Know therefore that the Lord your God, he is God, the faithful God, which keep covenant and mercy with them who love him and keep his commandments to a thousand generations; And repay them who hate him to their face, to destroy them: he will not be slack to him that heats him; he will repay him to his face (Deuteronomy 7:9-10).

10.   TO WHAT WAS ISRAEL TOLD TO PAY SPECIAL ATTENTION?

You shall therefore keep the commandments, and the statutes, and the judgments, which I command you this day, to do them. Wherefore it shall come to pass, if you hearken to these judgments, and keep unto you the covenant and the mercy which he swore unto your fathers (Deuteronomy 7:11-12).

HOW WOULD ISRAEL BE BLESSED

11.   HOW WOULD ISRAEL BE BLESSED BY OBEYING GOD?

And he will love you, and bless you, and multiply you: he will also bless the fruit of your womb, and the fruit of your land, your com, and your wine, and your oil, the increase of your kina, and the flocks of your sheep, in the land which he swore unto your fathers to give you. You shall be blessed above all people: there shall not be male or female barren among you, or among your cattle. And the Lord will take away from you all sickness, and will put none of the evil diseases of Egypt, which you know, upon you; but will lay them upon all them, that hate you (Deuteronomy 7:13-15).

12.   HOW WOULD OTHER GOD'S HURT ISRAEL'S RELATIONSHIP WITH GOD?
And you shall consume all the people which the Lord your God shall deliver you, your eye shall have no pity upon them: neither shall you serve their gods; for that will be a snare unto you (Deuteronomy 7:16).

13.   WHAT FEARFUL QUESTION DO THE PEOPLE OF ISRAEL ASK?
If you shall say in your heart, these nations are more than I; how can I dispossess them? (Deuteronomy 7:17).

14.   HOW WAS ISRAEL TOLD NOT TO FEAR THE OTHER NATIONS?
You shall not be afraid of them: but shall well remember what the Lord your God did unto Pharaoh, and unto all the Egypt; The great temptations which your eyes saw, and the signs, and the wonders, and the mighty hand, and the stretched out arm, whereby the Lord your God brought you out: so shall the Lord your God do unto all the people of whom you are afraid. Moreover the Lord your God will send the hornet among them, until they that are left, and hide themselves from you, be destroyed (Deuteronomy 7:18-20)

CHARACTERISTICS OF GOD

15.   WHAT CHARACTERISTICS OF GOD ARE DESCRIBED IN THIS PASSAGE?
You shall not be affrighted at them: for the Lord your God is among you, a mighty God and terrible (Deuteronomy 7:21).

16.   HOW WAS ISRAEL PROMISED BY GOD TO DRIVE OUT THE OTHER NATIONS?
And the Lord your God will put out those nations before you by little and little: you may not consume them at once, lest the beasts of the field increase upon you. But the Lord your God shall deliver them unto you, and shall destroy them with a mighty destruction, until they be destroyed. And he shall deliver their name from under heaven: there shall no man be able to stand before you, until you have destroyed them (Deuteronomy 7:22-24)

17.   WHAT WAS ISRAEL TOLD TO DO WITH THE PAGAN GODS?
The graven images of their gods shall you burn with fire: you shall not desire the silver or gold that is on them, not take it unto you, lest you be snared therein: for it is an abomination to the Lord your God. Neither shall you bring an abomination into your house, lest you be a cursed thing like it: but you shall utterly detest it, and you shall utterly abhor it; for it is a cursed thing (Deuteronomy 7:25-26).

GET IT:

There are ethical questions asked that you would have to get from reading the Scripture.

18.   What do you think others think of when they hear the word "IDOL?"

19.   What is the danger of Christians following idols?

20.   In what ways do people sometimes make idols out of other people?

21.   How to impersonal idols ruin a personal relationship with God?

22.   What type of statement did God make by asking for the complete destruction of idols?

23.   How does the warning God gave Israel about idols relate to us today?

24.   How is God able to drive out the idols in a person's life?

APPLY IT:

25.   What is an idol you need to forsake in order to follow God faithfully?

26.   How can you bolster your confidence in the great and awesome power of God?

WORSHEET: Sexual Relations (Leviticus 18 & 20)

Unlawful Sexual Relations (Leviticus 18:1-30)

TOPICS:
Culture, Family, Homosexuality, Punishment, Relationships, Sex

Marriages between Israelites were directed by law, and everyone having committed incest. The people of Israel were not to marry anyone that was closely related to avoid relationship in a way to marry legally that involving incest with each other in the family. In addition, priests were forbidden to marry prostitutes and divorced women. Daughters who inherited their father's possessions had to marry within their tribe or lose their inheritance.

1.   What makes people nervous about going on a blind date?

_____

2.   What parts of American society exploit sex?

_____

EXPLORE IT:

THE LORD SPAKE UNTO MOSES, SAYING, Speak unto the children of Israel, and say unto them, I am the Lord your God.

[3]   After the doings of the land of Egypt, wherein you dwelt, shall you not do: and after the doings of the land of Canaan, wither I bring you, shall you not do: neither shall you walk in their ordinances.

[4]   You shall do my judgments, and keep mine ordinances, to walk therein: I am the Lord your God.

[5]   You shall therefore keep my statute, and my judgment: which if a man does, he shall live in them: I am the Lord.

[6]   None of you shall approach to any that is near of kin to him, to uncover their nakedness: I am the Lord.

[7]   The nakedness of (your father), (or the nakedness of your mother), shall you not uncover: (she is your mother),

[8]   The nakedness of your father's wife shall you not uncover, it is your father's wife,

[9]   The nakedness of your sister), (the daughter of your father), (or daughter of your mother), (whether she be born at home), (or born abroad) (even their nakedness you shall not uncover), la-the (nakedness of your son's daughter), (or of your daughter's daughter), even their nakedness you shall not uncover: heir's is your own nakedness.

[11]   The nakedness of (your father's wife's) (daughter, begotten of your father), (she is your sister), you shall not uncover her nakedness.

[12]   *You shall not uncover the nakedness of your (father's sister): (she is your father near kinswoman).*

[13]   *You shall not uncover the nakedness of (your mother's sister): she is your mother's near kinswoman.*

[14]   *You shall not uncover the nakedness of your (father's brother), (you shall not approach to his wife): (she is your aunt).*

[15]   *You shall not uncover the nakedness of your (daughter in law:) she is (your son's wife).*

[16]   *You shall not uncover the nakedness of (your brother's wife:) it is your brother's nakedness.*

[17]   *You shall not uncover the nakedness of a (woman and her daughter), neither shall you take her (son's daughter) or her(daughter's daughter) to uncover her nakedness; for (they are her near kinswoman): 18-neither shall you take a (wife to her sister,) (to vex her), (to uncover her nakedness beside the other in her life time). 19-also you shall not approach unto a woman to uncover her nakedness, (as long as she is put apart for her uncleanness).*

[20]   *Moreover you shall (not lie carnally with you (neighbor's wife), to defile yourself with her.*

[21]   *And you shall not (let any of your seed) (pass through the fire to Molech) (neither shall you) (profane the name of your God: (I am the Lord).*

[22]   *You shall not *lie with *(mankind), *as with *(womankind): *(it is abomination).*

[23]   *Neither shall (you lie with any beast) to defile yourself therewith: neither shall any woman stand before a beast to lie down thereto: it is confusion.*

[24]   *Defile not yourselves in any of these things: for in all the nations are defiled which I cast out before you:*

[25]   *And the land is defiled: therefore I do visit the iniquity thereof upon it, and the land itself vomited out her inhabitants.*

[26]   *You shall therefore keep my statues and my judgment, and shall not commit any of these abominations; neither any of your own nation, nor any stranger that sojourn among you:*

[27]   *For all these abominations have the men of the land done which were before you, and the land is defiled;)*

[28] -   *That the land spewed not you out also, when you defile it, as it spewed out the nations that were before you.*

[29]   *For whosoever shall commit any of these abominations, even the souls that commit them shall be cut off from among their people.*

[30]   *Therefore shall you keep mine ordinance, that you commit not anyone of these abominable customs, which were committed before you, and that you defile not yourselves therein: I am the Lord your God.*

3.   Who did God say He was to the Israelites? (Leviticus 18:1-2)

_____

4.   Whose practices did God tell the Israelites not to follow? (Leviticus 18:3-4)

_____

5.   What happens to the man who obeys the laws of the Lord? (Leviticus 18:5)

_____

6.   Who was allowed to have sexual relations with close relatives? (Leviticus 18:6)

_____

7.   What did God say about having sexual relations with one's mother? (Leviticus 18:7-8).

_____

8.   What was God's command to the Israelites regarding sex with one's sister? (Leviticus 18:9)

_____

Nakedness of Your Sister

9.   Why were the Israelites not allowed to have sexual relations with grandchildren? (Leviticus 18:10)

_____

10.   Who is the daughter of "your father's father's wife"? (Leviticus 18:11)

_____

11.   What were the Israelites told about sexual relations with close relatives? (Leviticus 18:12-14)

_____

12.   Why were the Israelites not to have sex with daughters-in-law? (Leviticus 18: IS)

_____

13.   Who is dishonored if an Israelite had sexual relations with his brother's wife? (Leviticus 18:16)

_____

14.   What were some of the regulations regarding sexual relations? (Leviticus 18:17-20)

_____

15.   Whose name was profaned when children were sacrificed to Molech? (Leviticus 18:21)

_____

16.   What was considered detestable to the Lord? (Leviticus 18:22)

_____

17.   With what were men and women told not to have sexual relations? (Leviticus 18:23)

_____

18.   Why did the Lord tell the Israelites not to defile themselves? (Leviticus 18:24-30)

_____

Protecting Family Members

GET IT:

19.   How does God want to protect family members?

_____

20.   What are some of the benefits of honoring God by making good sexual decisions?

_____

21.   How is sex such a powerful force in our society?

_____

22.   In what way do God's laws about sexuality and sexual relations promote a positive view of sexuality?

_____

23.   What types of abuse go on in families who don't honor god's laws on sexuality?

_____

24.   What makes it important to talk to our children about their sexuality?

_____

25.   If people honored God with their bodies, what would they gain?

_____

26.   How does God want us to be different from the rest of our world?

_____

27.   What does God promise to those who confess their sins to?

_____

APPLY IT:

28.   How can you honor God today in the area of your sexuality?

_____

29.   Who is someone you can talk to this week to help you be accountable to make God-honoring sexual decisions?

_____

Sexual Relations (Leviticus 18:1-30)

WHAT PARTS OF AMERICAN SOCIETY EXPLOIT SEX?

SCRIPTURE CONCERNING SEXUALITY FROM A SPRITUAL POINT A VIEW (Leviticus 18:1-30):

THE LORD SPAKE UNTO MOSES, SAYING, Speak unto the children of Israel, and say unto them, I am the Lord your God.

[3]   After the doings of the land of Egypt, wherein you dwelt, shall you not do: and after the doings of the land of Canaan, wither I bring you, shall you not do: neither shall you walk in their ordinances.

[4]   You shall do my judgments, and keep my ordinances, to walk therein: I am the Lord your God.

[5]   You shall therefore keep my statute, and my judgment: which if a man does, he shall live in them: I am the Lord.

[6]   None of you shall approach to any that is near of kin to him, to uncover their nakedness: I am the Lord.

[7]   The nakedness of (your father), (or the nakedness of your mother), shall you not uncover: (she is your mother),

[8]   The nakedness of your father's wife shall you not uncover, it is your father's wife,

[9]   The nakedness of your sister), (the daughter of your father), (or daughter of your mother), (whether she be born at home), (or born abroad) (even their nakedness you shall not uncover),

[10]   The (nakedness of your son's daughter), (or of your daughter's daughter), even their nakedness you shall not uncover: heir's is your own nakedness.

[11]   The nakedness of (your father's wife's) (daughter, begotten of your father), (she is your sister), you shall not uncover her nakedness.

[12]   You shall not uncover the nakedness of your (father's sister): (she is your father near kinswoman).

[13]   You shall not uncover the nakedness of (your mother's sister): she is your mother's near kinswoman.

[14]   You shall not uncover the nakedness of your (father's brother), (you shall not approach to his wife): (she is your aunt).

[15]   You shall not uncover the nakedness of your (daughter in law:) she is (your son's wife).

[16]   You shall not uncover the nakedness of (your brother's wife:) it is your brother's nakedness.

[17]   You shall not uncover the nakedness of a (woman and her daughter), neither shall you take her (son's daughter) or her(daughter's daughter) to uncover her nakedness; for (they are her near kinswoman): [18] neither shall you take a (wife to her sister,) (to vex her), (to uncover her nakedness beside the other in her life time). [19]-also you shall not approach unto a woman to uncover her

nakedness, (as long as she is put apart for her uncleanness).

[20]   Moreover you shall (not lie carnally with you (neighbor's wife), to defile yourself with her.

[21]   And you shall not (let any of your seed) (pass through the fire to Molech) (neither shall you) (profane the name of your God: (I am the Lord).

[22]   You shall not *lie with *(mankind), *as with *(womankind): *(it is abomination).

[23]   Neither shall (you lie with any beast) to defile yourself therewith: neither shall any woman stand before a beast to lie down thereto: it is confusion.

[24]   Defile not yourselves in any of these things: for in all the nations are defiled which I cast out before you:

[25]   And the land is defiled: therefore I do visit the iniquity thereof upon it, and the land itself vomited out her inhabitants.

[26]   You shall therefore keep my statues and my judgment, and shall not commit any of these abominations; neither any of your own nation, nor any stranger that sojourn among you:

[27]   For all these abominations have the men of the land done which were before you, and the land is defiled ;)

[28] -   That the land spewed not you out also, when you defile it, as it spewed out the nations that were before you.

[29]   For whosoever shall commit any of these abominations, even the souls that commit them shall be cut off from among their people.

[30]   Therefore shall you keep mine ordinance, that you commit not anyone of these abominable customs, which were committed before you, and that you defile not yourselves therein: I am the Lord your God.

This conclude the unlawful sexual relation that require of the Lord God the creator of heaven and earth. This gives a clear picture of why things are the way they are in our social world. It is all because we are not living by the laws of the creator of the heaven and earth who set things in place from the beginning in a way that the people who were to come could live in peace and happiness without having abominations to defile us, not that we can't help it; it is more likely that we aren't committed enough to his will in a way of being kept by him. *Greater is he who is in us then he who is in the world.* It seems as though it is he who's in the world who is keeping us than he who is within.

We discussed how marriages between Israelites were directed by law, and some relationships were outlawed. In addition, priests were forbidden to marry any divorced women. At this time we will go into the consequences of disobedience.

OPEN IT: Write your answers on the lines below.

1.   What is your favorite childhood memory?

_____

2.   What do most people you know think is God's view of sex? (Positive OR Negative)

_____

3.   Why do you think some people are drawn into the occult?

_____

Leviticus 20:1-27

<u>EXPLORE IT</u>:

4.   What happened to people who gave their children to Molech? (Leviticus 20:1-2)

_____

5.   Why were the consequences so severe to those who gave their children to Molech? (Leviticus 20:3)

_____

6.   When people closed their eyes to what was happening to children, what resulted? (Leviticus 20:4-5)

_____

7.   What did God think of people who listened to spirits and mediums? (Leviticus 20:6)

_____

8.   Why was Israel told to be holy? (Leviticus 20:7-8)

_____

9.   What are the consequences of cursing a mother and father? (Leviticus 20:9)

_____

10.   What are the consequences of having unlawful sexual relations? (Leviticus 20:10-13)

_____

Wickedness of Man

Underline the correct answer to the question according to the Scripture which will be provided the question.

11.   WHY DID GOD FORBID A MAN TO MARRY BOTH A WOMAN AND HER MOTHER?

And if a man takes a wife and her mother, it is wickedness: they shall be burnt with fire, both he and they that there is no wickedness among you (Leviticus 20:14).

12.   WHAT WAS THE LAW CONCERNING SEXUAL CONTACT WITH ANIMALS?

And if a man lies with a beast, he shall surely be put to death: and you shall slay the beast. And if a woman approach unto any beast, and lie down thereto, you shall kill the woman, and the beast: they shall surely be put to death; their blood shall be upon them (Leviticus 20:15-16).

13.   HOW MIGHT A MAN DISHONOR HIS SISTER?
And if a man shall take his sister, his father's daughter, or his mother's daughter, and see her nakedness; and she see his nakedness; it is a wicked thing, and they shall be cut off in the sight of their people. He has uncovered his sister's nakedness. He shall bear his iniquity (Leviticus 20: 17)

14.   WHAT RESTRICTION DID GOD PLACE ON A MAN'S SEXUAL RELATION WITH A WOMAN DURING HER PERIOD?
And if a man shall lie with a woman having her sickness, and shall uncover her nakedness; he has discovered her fountain, and she has uncovered the fountain of her blood: and both of them shall be cut off from among their people (Leviticus 20: 18)

15.   HOW WERE RELATIVES DISHONORED BY UNLAWFUL SEXUAL RELATIONSHIP?
And you shall not uncover the nakedness of your mother's sister, nor of your father's sister: for he uncovered his near kin: they shall bear their iniquity. 20 And if a man shall lie with his uncle's wife, he has uncovered his uncle's nakedness: they shall bear their sin, they shall die childless. 21 And if a man shall take his brother's wife, it is an unclean thing: he has uncovered his brother's nakedness; they shall be childless (Leviticus 20:20- 21)

16.   WHAT DID GOD PROMISE ISRAEL FOR ABIDING BY HIS LAWS?
You shall therefore keep all my statutes, and all my judgments, and do them: that the land, whither I bring you to dwell therein, spew you not out. 23 And you shall not walk in the manners of the nation, which I cast out before you: for they committed all these things, and therefore I abhorred them. 24 But I have said unto you, you shall inherit their land, and I will give it unto you to possess it, a land that flow with milk and honey: I am the Lord your God, which has separated you from other people (Leviticus 20:22-24)

17.   WHAT TYPE OF DISTINCTION DID GOD ASK THE PEOPLE TO MAKE BETWEEN CERTAIN ANIMALS?
You shall therefore put difference between clean beasts and unclean, and between unclean fowls and clean: and you shall not make your souls abominable by beast, or by fowl, or by any manner of living thing that creep on the ground, which I have separated from you as unclean (Leviticus 20:25)

18.   WHY DID THE LORD SET THE NATION OF ISRAEL APART FROM THE OTHER NATIONS?
And you shall be holy unto me: for I the Lord am holy, and have severed you from other people, that you should be mine (Leviticus 20:26)

19.   HOW WERE MEDIUMS AND SPIRITISTS PUT TO DEATH?

A man also or woman that has a familiar spirit, or that is a wizard, shall surely be put to death: they shall stone them with stones: their blood shall be upon them (Leviticus 20:27).

GET IT:
20. What are certain practices in our world today that God says are detestable?
21. How do you think God feels when he sees children destroyed by their parents?
22. What makes it wrong when we close our eyes to evil?
23. How can God's people make a difference in this world by standing up for righteousness?
24. What did God want to guard against by forbidding unlawful sexual practices?
25. How can bad sexual decisions lead to severe consequences?
26. What are positive ways we can protect and nurture our children?

WHAT DOES THIS PASSAGE SAY
27. What does this passage say about God's love for children?
28. Why is it dangerous to dabble in fortune-telling?

APPLY IT:

29. What can you do to stand up for the right of innocent children?
30. In which of your present circumstances do you need to show child-like faith?

This conclude this passage of all incestuous relationships were outlawed in (Leviticus 20:22-24). In the addition, priests were forbidden to marry prostitutes or divorced women (Leviticus 21:7,13-14), are about daughters who inherited their father's possessions had to marry within their tribe or lose their inheritance.

WORKSHEET: Rules for Priests (Leviticus 21:13-24)

TOPICS:
Acceptance, Follow, Marriage, Priorities, Privilege, Respect

OPEN IT:
1.   What are some things people do to develop a healthy sense of pride?
2.   Why is the example and life-style of leaders important?
3.   What happens when there is a breakdown in leadership in business and politics?

THE EXCEPTIONS OF THE PRIESTS (LEVITICUS 21:7, 13-14)
4.   In verses 7, 13, and 14 are the exceptions of the priest which is given for   True/False
        ceremonial uncleanness:

5.   Was a priest to take a wife that is a whore, or were they to take a woman   True/False
        that has been put away from her husband:

6.   Is this woman who has been put away from her husband, should a priest   True/False
        take her as his wife

7.   Is it because this priest is holy unto God is why he shouldn't take this   True/False
        woman as his wife?

8.   Should the priest take a wife in her virginity   True/False

9.   Why should the priest take a woman in her virginity? Is it because of   True/False
        him being holy unto God?

10.   Does the law require that a priest take a woman in her virginity?   (a) / (b)
        (a) that this is a requirement of God? or (b) requirements of the law

11.   The high priest different from the other priest because of the anointing   True/False
        oil was poured upon him?

12.   Was this priest who were among the brethren whose head the anointing   True/False
        oil was poured upon?

13.   Pouring the anointing oil upon the priest a form of consecrating the   True/False
        priest?

14.   When consecrating, the priest should he have on the garments of a   True/False
        priest?

15. The priest should uncover his head that anointed   True/False

What Did God Promise?

16. The garment the priest puts on should cover his head   True/False
17. What were the marriage regulations for a priest? He was to take a wife in   True/False
    her virginity:

18. He was not to take, (a) a divorced woman or (b) a harlot   (a) / (b)

19. It was ok for him to profane his seed among his people   True/False

20. The priests were sanctified by the Lord God: True/False

21. If the priest married a harlot or a divorced woman he would be   True/False
    profaning himself before God,

22. why would he be profane, (a) because of the holiness of God, or (b)   (a) / (b)
    because God has sanctified him

What Moses Told Aaron Regarding Physical Defects of Descendants

(Leviticus 21:16-24)

[16] And the Lord speak unto Moses, saying [17] Say unto Aaron, saying, whosoever he be of your (seed in their generation) has any (blemish), let him (not approach) to offer the (bread) of his God. [18] For whatsoever man he be that has a (blemish), he shall not (approach): a (blind man), or (a lame), or he who has (a flat nose), or anything superfluous, or (a man that is broken-footed), or (broken-handed), [20] (or crook-back), or (a dwarf), or that has (a blemish in his eye), or be scurvy, or scabbed, (or has his stones broken). [21] (no man that has a blemish of the seed of Aaron the priest shall come nigh) to (offer the offerings of the Lord made by fire): (he has a blemish).(he shall not come nigh to offer the bread of his God). [22] (He shall eat the bread of his God), (both of the most holy), (and of the holy). [23] (only he shall not go in unto the evil), (nor come nigh unto the altar), (because he has a blemish).(that he profanes not my sanctuaries): (for I the Lord do sanctify them). [24] And Moses (told it unto Aaron), and to (his son), and (unto all the children of Israel) (Leviticus 21:16-24).

23   Leviticus 22:1-3: The Lord spoke unto Moses, saying speak unto Aaron   True/False
     and his sons, say to them who they are to separate themselves from the

holy things of the children of Israel, and that they profane not His holy name in those things which they hallow unto me: I am the Lord

24. Leviticus 22:3: the Lord asked Moses to say unto them, whosoever he be of all your seed among your generation, that go unto the holy things, which the children of Israel hallow unto the Lord, having his uncleanness upon him, that soul shall be cut off from my presence: I am the Lord,   True/False

25. Why were the priest to keep the regulations of the Lord, could it be because they were not able to bear the sins for it   True/False

26. If the priest profane the will of God what would happen? Explain

27. Did the Lord sanctify the priest   True/False

28. Who was authorized to eat the sacred offerings, was it to be a stranger   True/False

29. Was a journeying priest or an hired servant able to eat the holy thing   True/False

30. Leviticus 22:10: There shall no stranger eat of the holy thing: a sojourner of the priest, or an hired servant, shall not eat of the holy thing   True/False

31. Why aren't they able to eat the holy thing? Explain

Things Were Not to Be Done

<u>MOSES SPEAKS TO AARON</u>:

32. Aaron's seed in his generation that had any blemish, he was not to approach to offer the bread of his God   True/False

33. Whatsoever man he be that have a _____, he shall not _____

34. Leviticus 21:18: What kind of person should not do (a) blind man or (b) a lame, or (c) he who has a flat nose)   (a) / (b) / (c)

35. Was other men able to eat the holy thing.   True/False
If true, what kind of person?_____

36. What was the priest able to do for the man with the broken-foot or broken-hand able to do for these persons? Explain:

37. Leviticus 22:12: If the priest's daughter also be married unto a stranger, she may not eat of an offering of the holy things of the Lord   True/False

38. Leviticus 22:14: If a man eat of the holy thing unwittingly, then he shall put the fifth part thereof unto it, and shall give it unto the priest with the holy thing   True/False

Leviticus 22, can you see the coming of Jesus through the view point of the prophet? *And the priest shall wave them with the bread of the first-fruits for a wave offering before the Lord, with the two lambs: they shall be holy to the Lord for the priest.*

Can you see the Lamb of God in this? In the Old Testament whenever a lamb is being sanctified it's a show of the blood of Jesus Christ which redeemed the people of God. Jesus said he is the bread of life, he is that bread came down from heaven of the Father.

And you shall proclaim on the selfsame day, that it may be an holy convocation unto you: you shall do no servile work therein: it shall be a statute forever in all your dwellings throughout your generation (Leviticus 23 :21).

WORKSHEET: Samson's Marriage (Judges 14:1-20)

TOPICS:
Abilities, Accomplishment, Affections, Bargaining, Conflict, Disobedience, Intimidation, Love, Marriage, Parents, Rebellion, Strength, Temptation, Unfaithfulness, Wives

OPEN IT:

1.   What are some of the degree of people expertness in using to persuade others?

2.   What methods have you used to convince someone to do something he or she didn't want to do?

3.   How have you ever been persuaded to do something you didn't want to do?

CHOOSING THE BRIDE: In the Old Testament time, the parents chose the mate for their son, the primary reason for this was that the bride became part of the clan. Although they were married and became "one flesh, the couple remained under the authority of the bridegroom's father. The parents chose someone who would best fit into their clan and work harmoniously with her mother-in-law and sister-in-law. Sometimes the parents consulted with their children to see if they approved of the choice of mates being made for them. For example, Rebekah was asked if she wanted to marry Isaac. Samson demanded that a certain girl be acquired for him.

REFERENCE TO SAMSON'S MARRIAGE: *And they said, we will call the damsel, and enquire at her mouth. And they called Re-bash, and said unto her, will you go with this man? And she said I will go (Genesis 24:57-58).*

Reading about Rebekah in Genesis 24:38-40; 43-45; 58 will give some understanding concerning the reasons parents chose their children's mates. They believed in looking to God as well as going on their own in choosing. Samson demanded that a certain girl be acquired for him. Although his parents protested, they completed the marriage contract for Samson. Samson asked his father and mother to get this woman he saw in Timnath who was the daughter of the Philistines. His father and mother didn't seem to like that too much. They asked him if there wasn't a woman among the brethren, or among all the people, that he could take as a wife rather than getting one that's uncircumcised who is a damsel. Samson said unto his father, Get her for me; for she pleases me well. But his father and his mother knew not that it was of the Lord that he sought an occasion against the Philistines, for at that time the Philistines had dominion over Israel. Samson didn't tell his father and mother he was going down to Timnath to talk with the woman. She pleased Samson well (Judges 14:1-4,15-16). Frequently people married at a young age, a fact which made the parents' choice a practical matter.

By the New Testament times, the Jewish leaders had decided to establish a minimum age for which a marriage contract should be drawn up. The age was set at 13 for boys and 12 years of age for girls. Even if the young wife lost her husband in war or accident, she remained within the clan and was wed to her brother-in-law or the next of kin. This arrangement is known as levirate marriage, it is basis for the story of Ruth and Boaz (Deuteronomy 25:5-10; Ruth 3:13; 4:1-12).

CONCEPT OF LOVE: Romance before marriage was not unknown in Old Testament times; it played a minor role in the life of teenagers of that era. They did not marry the person they loved; they learned to love the mate they married. Love seemed to have began at marriage. When Isaac married Rebekah, the Bible records that "she became his wife, and he loved her" (Genesis 24:67)

A Self-Centered Marriage

Samson went down to a place call Tim'nath, there he saw a woman the daughter of the Philistines; he came up, and told his father and mother, concerning her and said, I have seen a woman in Tim'nath the daughter of the Philistines: so he asked the father to get her for him to be his wife. The father and his mother said unto Samson, is there never a woman among the daughters of your brethren, or among all my people, and you go to take a wife of the uncircumcised Philistines? Samson said to his father, get her for me; she please me well.

BIBLICAL TIMES MARRIAGE: A mutual pledge for marriage was a binding agreement that set the young woman apart for the young man. The agreement was voided only by death or divorce; one could not get out of the betrothal in any other way; once you become engaged to be married to someone, that's it you can't get out of it other than by death or divorce. When Joseph discovered that Mary was pregnant, he did not want to make a "public example" of her; instead, he decided to divorce her secretly, the Bible say put her away: the word being translated divorce. Although he didn't carry out that he decided, because an angel of the Lord appeared unto him in a dream saying Joseph son of David, fear not to take unto you Mary your wife: for that which is conceived in her is of the Holy Ghost (Matthew 1 :20). During the engagement period, the bridegroom had certain privileges. If war was declared, he was exempt from military duty. He also knew that his bride-to-be was protected by Mosaic Law.

And what man is there had betrothed a wife, and had not taken her? Let him go and return unto his house, lest he died in the battle, and another man takes her (Deuteronomy 20:7).

Protection of the Bride-to-Be

BY THE MOSAIC LAW: Because of the Mosaic Law brides-to-be were protected. If any other man should rape her, the act was treated as adultery; and the offender was punished accordingly. This was considered a more serious crime then the rape of a girl not yet betrothed, if she have not made a commitment to be married, and should be raped, it is more serious than otherwise.

REFERENCE TO ADULTERY: If a damsel that is a virgin be betrothed unto an husband, and a man find her in the city, and lie with her; Then you shall bring them both out unto the gate of that city, and you shall stone them with stones that they die; the damsel, because she cried not, being in the city, and the man, because he had humbled his neighbor's wife: so you shall put away evil from among you.

MAN FINDS A BETROTHED DAMSEL: Betrothed is being translated to a person engaged to be married: Scripture; But id a man find a woman who is engaged to be married and a man find her in the field, and the man force her, and lie with her then the man only that lay with her shall die.

ABOUT THE DAMSEL: But unto the damsel you shall do nothing. There is in the damsel no sin worthy of death: for as when a man reset against his neighbor, and slay him, even so is this matter.

THE DAMSEL IS FOUND IN THE FIELD: *For he found her in the field, and the person who was engaged, the damsel cried, and there was none to save her* (Deuteronomy 22:23-29).

WORKSHEET: Teaching About Marriage

Teaching New Testament Marriage

The New Testament does not contradict the teachings about marriage in the Old. Most marriage teaching in the New comes from Jesus and the apostle Paul. Jesus' first miracle occurred in Canal in Galilee when He and His disciples were attending a wedding where he changes water to wine. There our Lord Jesus Christ gave His blessing and sanction to the institution of marriage.

REFLECTION CONCERNING MARRIAGE (John 2: 1-11)

1.	John 2:1: Was the marriage on the third day?	Yes / No
2.	John 2:1: Were Jesus and his mother there?	True / False
3.	John 2:2: Were Jesus and his disciples called to the marriage?	Yes / No
4.	John 2:3: When they had no wine, what did Jesus' mother say?	
5.	John 2:4: When Jesus answered her, what did he say	
6.	John 2: 5: What did the mother say to the servants?	
7.	John 2:6: There were six water pots of stone, after the manner of the purifying of the Jews, containing two or three firkins apiece	True / False
8.	John 2:9: What happen when the ruler of the feast had tasted the water?	
9.	Was it made wine?	
10.	Did the servants know where the water came from?	Yes / No
11.	John 2:11: After Jesus manifested forth his glory, did his disciple believed on him	
12.	Why did Jesus keep the good wine until now?	

Jesus Speaks about Marriage and Divorce

When Jesus was asked about marriage and divorce, he quoted two passages from Genesis. *Have you not read that He who made them at the beginning made the male and female; and said, for this reason a man shall leave his father and mother and be joined to his wife, and the two shall become one flesh? So then, they are no longer two but one flesh. Therefore what God has joined together, let not no man separate* (Matthew 19:4-6).

Jesus taught that marriage was the joining together of two people so they become "one flesh." Not only did God acknowledge the marriage, He also joined the couple together.

Let No Man Separate (Genesis 1:27; 2:24) (Matthew 19:4-6)

1.   <u>God Created Man and Woman</u>: *God created man in his own image, in the image of God created he him; male and female created he him* (Genesis 1:27).

2.   <u>Man Shall Leave His Father and Mother</u>: Therefore shall a man leave father and his mother, and shall cleave unto his wife: and they shall be one flesh (Genesis 2:24).

3.   <u>The Marriage was Blessed</u>: *Male and female created he them; and blessed them, and called their name Adam, in the day when they were created* (Genesis 5:2).

4.   <u>The Quotations of Jesus Concerning Marriage</u>: *And he answered and said unto them, Have you not read what he which made them at the beginning made them male and female, and said, for this cause shall a man leave father and mother, and shall cleave to his wife: and they twain shall be one flesh? Wherefore they are no more twain but one flesh. What therefore God has joined together, let not man put asunder* (Matthew 19:4-6).

<u>The Church at Corinth</u>: The church at Corinth struggled over a number of issues, including the proper view of marriage. In response to their questions. Paul gave an answer about marriage. From his answer it seems that three faulty ideas about marriage were prominent among some believers in the church.
1.   The first was that marriage was absolutely necessary in order to be a Christian.
2.   Another idea was that celibacy was superior to marriage.
3.   The third idea was that when a person became a Christian, all existing relationships such as marriage were dissolved.
When reading (1-Corinthians 7) with that as background, the following teaching seems to emerge.

Result in One's Salvation

<u>The Unbelievable Marriage</u>: The Bible speaks on the problem faced by a Christian believer whose spouse does not believe. If the unbelieving partner is willing to live with the Christian, then the Christian should not dissolve the marriage. Remaining with the unbeliever partner could result in their salvation.

An Underlining Partner: *For the unbelieving husband is sanctified by the wife, and the unbelieving wife is sanctified by the husband: else were your children unclean, but now are the holy 1-Corinthians 7: 14).*

In this letter to the Ephesians, Paul showed how a marriage relationship can best function. First he said, *Wives, submit yourselves unto your own husbands, as unto the Lord* (Ephesians 5:22).

What husband and wife team do you greatly admire? In your point a view, what one quality or ability sustains a marriage relationship? The model for the wife's submission is the church, which is subject to Christ. Husbands are to love their wives. The role that the husband plays is outlined by Jesus Christ, who loved His bride, the church, so much that he died for her.

Subject to Christ: *Therefore as the church is subject unto Christ, so let the wives be to their own husbands in everything* (Ephesians 5:24).

Outline By Jesus Christ, Who Loved the Church: **Husbands, love your wives, even as Christ also loved the church, and gave himself for it** (Ephesians 5:25).

Legal Dissolution of a Marriage

The Divine Ideal for Marriage: The divine ideal for marriage is clearly a life-long bond that unites husband and wife in "one flesh" having a marriage relationship.

For this Cause: *And said, for this cause shall a man leave father and mother, and shall cleave to his wife: and they twain shall be one flesh?* (Matthew 19:5).

The marriage union is a holy condition founded by God and is not to be dissolved at the will of man.

Marriage as a Holy Condition Founded by God: *Wherefore they are no more twain, but one flesh. What therefore God has joined together let not man put asunder* (Matthew 19: 6).

Separation of this bond displeased God and posed a serious expression of the intention of hurting Him. The Scripture says to grieve not the holy Spirit of God whereby you are sealed until the day of redemption.

Grieve Not the Holy Spirit of God: *And grieve not the Holy Spirit of God whereby you are sealed until the day of redemption* (Ephesians 4:30).

This ideal of dissolution which pose a serious social order in the physical life of marriages which is very treacherous within the family. The Bible teaches to not deal treacherously with the wife of your youth. For the Lord God hates divorce, for it covers one's garment with violence."

<u>Did Not He Make One</u>: *And did not he make one? Yet had he the residue of the spirit. And wherefore one? That he might seek a godly seed. Therefore take heed to your spirit, and let none deal treacherously against the wife of his youth. For the Lord, the God of Israel, said that he hate putting away: for one cover violence with his garment, said the Lord of hosts: therefore take heed to your spirit, that you deal not treacherously* (Malachi 2:15-16).

The Law of Moses Allowed Divorce

Moses law allowed man to divorce his wife when she is found "not having favor in the eyes of her husband, because he has found some uncleanness in her."

<u>When a Man Finds No Favor His Wife</u>: *When a man has taken a wife, and married, and it come to pass that she find no favor in his eyes, because he has found some uncleanness in her: then let him write her a bill of divorcement, and give it in her hand, and send her out of his house* (Deuteronomy 24:1).

In studying the Scripture I find this passage supports divorce, but that is not the case. It simply recognizes a practice that already existed in Israel. All four verses must be read to understand the point of the passage; it certainly is not suggesting that a man divorce his wife on a whim.

<u>Divorce was Permanent and Final</u>: Once divorced and remarried to others, they could never be remarried to each other again. This restriction was to prevent casual remarriage after a frivolous separation. My thoughts, just my thoughts, the intention was to make people think twice before divorcing.

<u>Her Former Husband</u>: *Her former husband, who sent her away, may not take her again to be his wife, after that she is defiled, for that is abomination before the Lord: and you shall not cause the land to sin, which the Lord your God gave you for an inheritance* (Deuteronomy 24:4).

This law was intended to discourage, rather than encourage divorce. A public document known as a "certificate of divorce" was granted to the woman. This permitted her the right to remarry without civil or religious sanction. Divorce could not be done privately.

Moses law called for severe penalties for certain types of "uncleanness." Adultery carried the death penalty by stoning for the woman. If a man believed his wife was not a virgin when he married her, he could have her judged by the elders of the city. If they find her guilty, she could be put to death.

Bound by the Law in Marriage

The Woman is Bound by Law: A man was allowed to divorce his wife. The wife was not allowed to divorce her husband for any reason. Legally the wife was bound to her husband as long as they both lived or until he divorced her.

The Wife is Bound: *The wife is bound by the law as long as her husband lives; but if her husband be dead, she is at liberty to be married to whom she will; only in the Lord* (1-Corinthians 7:3 9).

Jesus' day, confusion prevailed about the grounds for divorce. Even the rabbis could not agree on what constituted the "uncleanness" according to Moses law (Deuteronomy 24:1) where the man found no favor in his eyes because he had found some uncleanness in her. Followers of Rabbi Sammie felt adultery was the only grounds for divorce. The gospels record four statements by Jesus concerning divorce. In two of these he allowed divorce in the case of adultery. Jesus commented on the situation of both the woman and her husband: "whoever divorces his wife for any reason except sexual immorality causes her to commit adultery; and whoever marries a woman who is divorced commits adultery."

Divorce in Case of Adultery: *But I say unto you, that whosoever shall put away his wife, saving for the cause of fornication, cause her to commit adultery: and whosoever shall marry her that is divorced committee adultery* (Matthew 5:32).

The whole is here closed up with advice to widows. As long as the husband lives the wife is bound by the law, confined to one husband, and bound to continue and cohabit with him. The marriage-contract is for life; death only can annul the bond. But the husband being dead, she is at liberty to marry whom she will. According to this passage, there is no limitation by God's law to be married only for such a number of times. It is certain from this passage that second marriages are not unlawful; for then the widow could not be at liberty to marry whom she pleases, nor to marry a second time at all.

Jesus' Statements Made No Provision for Divorce

The whole land of Canaan was his parish, or diocese, and therefore he would visit every part of it, and gave instructions to those in the remotest corners of it. Wherever he was they flocked after him in crowds; they came to him again, as they had done when he had formerly been in these parts, and as he was wont, he taught them again.

Concerning Putting Away His Wife: *And he said unto them, whosoever shall put away his wife,*

130

and marry committed adultery against her. And if a woman shall put away her husband, and be married to another, she committed adultery (Mark 10:11-12).

<u>Both Persons Committed Adultery</u>: *Whosoever put away his wife, and married another, committee adultery and whosoever married her that is put away from her husband committee adultery* (Luke 16: 18).

We are mistaken if we imagine that the design of Christ's doctrine and holy religion of divine mysteries or to entertain us with notions of divine mercies. No, no, no, the divine revelation of both these in the gospel is intended to engage and quicken us to the practice of Christian duties, and as much as anyone thing, to the duty of beneficence and doing good to those who stand in need of anything that either we have or can do for them.

Do Jesus' statements allowing divorce for infidelity seem to be in conflict with biblical statements that seem to forbid it entirely? Mark and Luke write of Jesus in conversations with Pharisees about the Mosaic Law. This is reason enough to read the Scripture which must be read as it is being taught. *For precept must be upon precept, precept upon precept, line upon line, line upon line; here a little, and there a little, for with the tongue will he speak to this people* (Isaiah 28:10).

In doing so it will give a better understanding of Jesus' teachings as well as the Scripture pride as well. You will have a good understanding of divorce on grounds other than adultery which you read in (Deuteronomy 24:1-4).

Conversation with the Pharisees (Mark 10:2)

<u>Conversation with the Pharisees Regarding Divorce</u>: The Pharisees asked Jesus, "Is it lawful for a man to put away his wife?" This conversation is in Mark 10:2.

<u>Jesus Answered with a Question</u>: Mark 10 [V3] Jesus answered them with a question, **What did Moses command you?** [V4] The Pharisees said Moses suffered to write a bill of divorcement, and to put her away. [V5} Jesus then said unto them, **For the hardness of your heart he wrote you this precept.** [V6-9]Jesus went on to say, **From the beginning of the creation God made them male and female. For this cause shall a man leave his father and mother, and cleave to his wife; and they twain shall be one flesh; so then they are no more twain, but one flesh. What therefore God has joined together, let not man put asunder.**

In Mark10:10 the disciples ask the same questions as the Pharisees so Jesus explains to them, **[V11] Whosoever shall put away his wife, and marry another commits adultery against her. [V12] And if a woman shall put away her husband, and be married to another she commits adultery.** This concludes the conversation with the Pharisees and the matter with the disciples.

Preaching was Christ's constant practice; it was what He was used to, and wherever he came, he did as he was wont. His cures were to confirm His doctrine, and to recommend it, and His doctrine was to explain His cures, and illustrate them as He did with the Pharisees and the disciples in (Mark 10:5-12).

WORKSHEET: Divorce Concerning Scripture

Adultery, Creation, Law, Marriage, New Covenant, Separation, Teaching

1.   What do you think makes a marriage strong and lasting?

_____

2.   How do the people you work with view people with struggling or failed marriage?

_____

3.   What did this episode take place? (Mark 10:1)

_____

4.   What does this passage say about Christ's attitude toward his ministry? (Mark 10: 1)

_____

5.   Why did the Pharisees go to see Jesus? (Mark 10:2)

_____

6.   How did Jesus respond to the Pharisees' try to trick Jesus? (Mark 10:2)

_____

7.   How did Jesus respond to the Pharisees' question? (Mark 10:3)

_____

8.   Why do you think Jesus brought Moses into his discussion? (Mark 10:3)

_____

9.   What did Moses allow in the area of divorce? (Mark 10:4)

_____

10.   How did Jesus explain Moses' instructions? (Mark 10:5)

_____

11.   What do we learn about the Pharisees from Jesus' explanation of Moses' words?
(Mark 10:5)

_____

12.   How did Jesus explain the relationship between the Law and the will of God? (Mark
10:5-9)

13.   How did Jesus lend authority to His words? (Mark 10:6-9)

14.   What was God's original plan for marriage before sin entered the picture? (Mark 10:6-9)

15.   What is the meaning of "they are no longer two, but one"? (Mark 10:8)

OVERRRIDING PRINCIPLES:

16.   what overriding principle did Jesus want us to follow? (Mark 10:9)

17.   why did this topic come up a second time that day? (Mark 10:10)

18.   what specific instructions did Jesus give regarding divorce? (Mark 10:11-12)

19.   how did Jesus protect woman with his instructions? (Mark 10:11-12)

20.   How do you think the Pharisees expected to trick Jesus?

21.   What do we learn about human nature from Jesus' answer to the Pharisees' question? _____

22.   Why do you think Jesus referred back to the "Beginning of creation" in this debate?

23.   How could a person separate "what God has Joined together"?

24.   Why do you think the disciples asked Jesus about their question privately?

25. How should we view people with struggling or failed marriages?

_____

26. How can the church help people with struggling or failed marriages?

_____

27. How can the church help its members strengthen and even save their marriage?

_____

28. Why do you think so many marriages fail?

_____

WHAT CAN YOU DO TO STRENGTHEN?

29. What can you do to strengthen your own marriage or encourage a couple who is experiencing difficulty in this area?

_____

30. What attitude should we have toward marriage?

_____

31. How should a Christian's understanding of marriage differ from that of the popular image?

_____

32. How can a strong Christian marriage be an effective witness to unbelievers?

_____

APPLY IT:
33. What is one specific step you can take this week to show respect for the sanctity of marriage?

_____

34. For what couple cans you pray every day this week?

_____

Jesus' Main Point

In these statements divorce is contrary to God's plan for marriage and should never be taken lightly. Even though Moses Law allowed divorce, this was an exception granted under the law because of their "hardness" of heart (Mark 10:5). Jesus desired to put "teeth" into the law by declaring that, even if the divorced couple had not been sexually unfaithful to each other, they would commit adultery in God's sight if they now married other partners.

Symbolically Man and Woman Become One Flesh (Genesis 2:18-24)

In allowing divorce for the single reason of "immorality" or for custom sexual intercourse, Jesus' thought is clearly that a person dissolves his marriage by creating a sexual union with someone other than the marriage partner.

Such union violates the sacred "oneness" intended by God when He united Adam and Eve in the first marriage relationship. God's creative work was not complete until He made woman. He could have made her from the dust of the ground, as He made man.

God chose to make woman from the man's flesh and bone. He illustrated that in marriage man and woman symbolically become one flesh. This is a mystical union of the couple's hearts and lives.

God forms and equips men and women for various tasks. All these tasks lead to the same goal of honoring God. As it has been said before, man gives life to woman; woman gives life to the world. Each role carries exclusive privileges. There is no room for thinking that one sex is superior to the other. With this understanding we can understand that God gave marriage as a gift to Adam and Eve. They were created perfect for each other. Just as it should be today, instead, it seems if some have married for convenience, it was not brought about by any culture.

It is Not Good Man Should be Alone. (Genesis 2:18-21) *[18] And the Lord God said, it is not good that the man should be alone. I will make him a help meet for him. [19] And out of the ground the Lord God formed every beast of the field, and every fowl of the air, and brought them unto Adam to see what he would call them: and whatsoever Adam called every living creature that was the name thereof . [20] And Adam gave names to all cattle, and to the fowl of the air and to every beast of the field, but for Adam there was not found a help meet for him. [21] And the Lord God caused a deep sleep to fall upon Adam and he slept: and he took one of his ribs, and closed up the flesh instead thereof.*
I encourage you to read Genesis 2:22-25.

Sexual Unfaithfulness

Decree of Divorce. In this topic I would like to take just a little time out and talk about the case of sexual unfaithfulness. The decree of divorce simply reflects the fact that the marriage has already been broken. A man divorcing his wife for this cause does not "make her an adulteress." She is already is one. Divorce on the grounds of unfaithfulness usually frees the innocent partner to marry without incurring the guilt of adultery. Let us see what Jesus says about a matter of such a one.

Except it be for Fornication. *And I say unto you, whosoever shall put away his wife, except it be for fornication, and shall marry another, commits adultery. And whoso marry her which is put away commits adultery* (Matthew 19:9).

Here again we see the Pharisees temping Jesus concerning divorce. They are using the word translated "put her away." This is sometimes questioned. Jesus here in this verse is allowing divorce only if she is caught in adultery. He did not require it. On the contrary, He insisted that divorce disrupts God's plan for marriage and left the way open for repentance and forgiveness.

Paul seems to have agreement with Jesus' teaching on marriage and divorce. He dealt with things involving the marital conflict between believers and between a believer and a non-believer. In the case of two Christians Paul admonished them to follow the Lord's teachings and be reconciled. In and event, neither is to marry another.

Unto the Married. *And unto the married I command, yet not I, but the Lord, Let not (the wife depart from her husband): But and if she (departed), let her remain unmarried, or (be reconciled to her husband): and let not the husband put away his wife. But to the rest speak I, not the Lord: if any brother has a wife who believe not, and she be pleased to dwell with him, let him not put her away* (1-Corinthians 7:10-12)

Marriage Bond

Formalizing Divorce. Paul says that a Christian whose mate has abandoned the marriage should be free to formalize the divorce. *If the unbeliever departs let him depart. A brother or sister is not under bondage in such case: but God has called us to peace* (1-Coriinthians 7: 15).

A person who is using fornication or forming an unclean act in sexual intercourse has structure the order for the divorce, once that person has done such an act, that person has already committed adultery. The husband or wife who has done such an act is free to be put apart, but just in case they decide to forgive each other and ask the forgiveness of such an act and become reconciled it is pleasing to God.

Many (authorities) hold that phrase "not under bondage" to mean that a deserted Christian

spouse may lawfully go from divorce to remarriage. But other (scholars) disagree with this interpretation. Reason for these different beliefs is because they haven't studied the Scripture to the point of finding the real truth to the requirement of God for the marriage;
In any event, Paul encourages the believer to keep the marriage together in hopes that the unbelieving partner might be saved 1-Corinthians 7: 16)

<u>As an Illustration</u>. *As God has distributed to every man, as the Lord has called every one, so let him walk. And so ordain I in all churches. Is any man called being (circumcised)? Let him not become (uncircumcised) is any called in (uncircumcised)? Let him not be (circumcised). (Circumcision) is nothing, and (Uncircumcision) is nothing, but the keeping of the commandments of God. Let every man abide in the same calling wherein he was called* (1-Corinthians 7: 16-21).

The uncircumcised is one who is none believer; circumcised is the person who is saved. An unclean person is one who is uncircumcised; a circumcised person is clean. Jesus said *he who is washed is clean and need not wash his feet, but is clean*. Just before that saying, Jesus said, *if I wash not your feet, you have not part with me*.

From a spiritual point a view; reason with these sayings concerning a marriage, use these illustrations.

_____

_____

_____

WORKSHEET: MARRIAGE

TOPICS: Body, Freedom, Immorality, Marriage, Ministry, Morality, Prayer, Sex, Sin, Singleness, Slavery, Temptation, Unbelievers

1.   What couple have you met recently that displays the ingredients of a good marriage?

_____

2.   What to you is good and bad about remaining single?

_____

3.   1-Corinthians 7:1-40 gives us what guiding principles about marriage does God wants us to know?

_____

4.   According 1-Corinthians 7:2: why should "each man should have his own wife?"

_____

5.   Who does a Christian's body belong if they are married, according to the Scripture?

_____

6.   What is more important than whether a person is married or single?

_____

7.   What is more important than whether a person is a slave or free?

_____

8.   What is one advantage in remaining single?

_____

you must read 1-Corinthians 7: 1-40 to attain the answers

WORKSHEET: Jesus Changes Water to Wine (John 2:1-11)

TOPICS: Assurance, Change, Confidence, Faith, Glory, Jesus Christ, Miracles, New Life, Spiritual Rebirth

OPEN IT:

1.   What are people interested in miraculous or supernatural events?

_____

2.   What makes an event miraculous or supernatural?

_____

3.   What supernatural or miraculous events have you witnessed?

_____

OPEN IT:

4.   Where did the wedding take place? (John 2:1)

_____

5.   Who was at the wedding? (John 2:1-2)

_____

6.   What did Jesus' mother say to him? (John 2:3)

_____

7.   What was Jesus' response to his mother? (John 2:4)

_____

8.   How did Jesus' mother respond to his reply? (John 2:5]

_____

9.   What were the water jars used for? (John 2:6)

_____

10.   What did Jesus tell the servants to do? (John 2:7)

_____

11.   To whom did the servants take the water? (John 2:8)

_____

12.   What happened to the water? (John 2:9)

_____

13.   What was the banquet master's response? (John 2:10)

_____

14.   Why did Jesus perform this miracle? (John 2:11)

_____

15.   How did Jesus' disciples respond to this miracle? (John2:11).

_____

MARRIAGE (JOHN 2:1-11): HOW HAVE YOU HAD FAITH

16.   How have you had faith in Jesus' power this week?

_____

17.   What is something you would like Jesus to change in your life

_____

18.   What recent miracle has Jesus done in your life?

_____

19.   How does Jesus reveal His glory to us today?

_____

20.   In what ways has Jesus transformed you into a new person?

_____

21.   How has Jesus given you a new life?

_____

22.   What things has Jesus done that have caused you to have faith in Him?

_____

23.   What is one specific habit or characteristic you will ask God to change in your life this week?

_____

24.   How will you enjoy today the new life Jesus has given you?

_____

25. In John 2:4 Jesus said unto his mother, woman what have I to do with you   True / False

26. When they wanted wine, the mother of Jesus said unto him, they have no wine   True / False

27. In John 2:3, If your wife should committee adultery, should you forgive her or put her away? If the woman you are going to marry should have a sexual intercourse could you or should you marry her? Give Scripture to support your answer: Yes / No

_____

WORKSHEET: Separation From God

These are YES or NO questions. Some of them you may have to get the answer from the Scripture. They are all of the Scripture and you must read the Scripture or this book in order to get the answer.

1. The marriage union is a holy condition founded by God — True / False

2. A person who is separated from this bond is displeasing to God — True / False

3. Does God need us? — True / False
    If false, give Scripture to support the answer:

4. Place the Scripture on the lines, there may be one or it could be all four

5. If a woman should committee adultery and her husband should not, according to the Old Testament Law, should he be put to death — True / False

6. Would God be pleased if the both of them could be reconciled back together? — Yes / No

7. Does divorce pose a serious threat to the social order of life? — True / False

8. According to Malachi 2:15: And let none deal treacherously with the wife of his youth? — True / False

9. Why did God create Adam? Was it because He needed him? — True / False
    Give the Scripture that support your answer:

10. God said I am holy. Did He say that so that we would be holy as He is holy? — True / False

11. When God said to go and multiply, and replenish the earth, did He mean that Eve was to do the same as being a woman? — True / False

12. Was Eve holy when she had her first child? — Yes / No

13. If she were holy when she had her first child, would that child have been holy? — True / False

14. When God put Adam out of the Garden of Eden, was Adam righteous? — True / False

15. Why did God put Adam out of the Garden Eden? Was it because he eats of the tree God asked him not to eat?   True / False

16. Or was it because he wouldn't put forth his hand and take the tree of life and eat also?
    It was only one of these reasons God put him out. Explain: True / False

17. Did God give Adam a chance to redeem himself because he disobeyed God's command?   True / False

18. Did it grieved God to his heart because he saw the imagination of the thoughts of man's heart was only evil continually?   True / False

19. Did it repented the Lord God that he had mad man on the earth   True / False

20. If Adam had obeyed God, would he have had the chance to live in the Garden of Eden in peace throughout his eternal life?   True / False

21. Because of the fall of Adam, is that the reason we sin?   True / False

22. Can we be made to sin?   True / False

23. Is it that we sin because of a mistake?   True / False

24. Or is it that we can't help it?   True / False

WORKSHEET: Legislation to Prevent Marriage Again

<u>CONCERNING DIVORCE</u>:

1. Is it displeasing to the Lord God for husband and wife to divorce?   True / False

2. It is said that divorce covers one's garment with violence.   True / False

3. In (Malachi 2:16), why did the Lord say he hate putting away one's wife? Explain?

4. The Lord of hosts said to take heed to your spirit, that you deal not   True / False
   treacherously

<u>THE KIND OF FRIEND YOU ARE</u>

TOPICS: Blessing, Covenant, Divorce, Evil, Faithfulness, God, Judgment, Justice, Listening, Marriage, Name, Oppressed, People, Prayer, Prophecy, Sin, Tithing, Unfaithfulness, Words

1. How would your closest friend describe the kind of friend you are?   True / False

2. In conversation do you tend to be a talker or a listener?

3. When do you feel most thankful for your blessings

4. Was the Law of Moses intended to discourage, rather than to   True / False
   encourage divorce?

5. A public document known as a certificate of divorce" was it for   True / False
   women only?

6. Does this kind of permitted her to right to remarry without civil or   True / False
   religious sanction?

7. If a person, man or woman, should have a sexual intercourse with another after marriage if neither one should make such an act, has either one has committed adultery should cause the other to committee adultery with whoever they should marry in the future? if you think they are or are not causing it, explain your reasons?

WORKSHEET: Adultery Carried the Death Penalty

1. Divorce could not be done privately?   True / False

2. Explain why couldn't divorce be done privately?

3. The Mosaic Law called for severe penalties for certain types of "uncleanness"?   True / False

4. If a man believed his wife was not a virgin when he married her, what could he have done unto his wife? When being in a marriage for some time and you learn that your wife was unclean, is this saying that she had a sexual intercourse with someone other than you?   True / False

5. If that be the case, according to the Mosaic Law, what could you do?

6. Was a man allowed to divorce his wife?   True / False

7. Was the wife allowed to divorce her husband for any reason?   True / False

8. Legal point was the wife was bond to her husband as long as they both lived?   True / False

9. 1- Corinthians 7:39: When is the wife is at liberty to marry another? is it at the death of him or after the divorce or is never?   True / False

10. 1- Corinthians 7:39: *The wife is bond by the law as long as her husband live; but if her husband be dead, she is at liberty; to be married to whom she will; only in the Lord.*   True / False

11. This is a Christian woman, she was to have been sexual faithful with her husband which made her clean but now unclean having she been with a man other than her husband, but if she be with another then she become unclean because of be adulteries?
Give Scripture reference: True / False

12. What constituted the "uncleanness?" is it finding no favor in one's eyes?   True / False

13. Is it good in the eyes of God that a Christian man and woman should divorce for whatever reason there might be?   True / False

WORKSHEET: Grounds for Divorce

<u>CONFUSION PREVAILED</u>:

1.   What constituted the divorce? Was it "uncleanness?"   True / False

2.   Was adultery the only grounds for divorce?   True / False

3.   What commitment do adults commonly make?

4.   What commitments do adults sometimes break?

5.   What causes people to break their commitments?

6.   What two things Jesus allowed divorce?

7.   Under line the one Jesus allowed:
(1-Adultery), (2-Commitment), (3-Divorce), (4-Faithfulness), (5-Marriage), (6-Remarriage), (7-Unfaithfulness), (8-Fornication).

8.   Does sexual immorality has anything to do with a person getting a divorce?   True / False

9.   Would you or could you divorce your wife because of sexual immorality? If No, give reason: Yes / No

10.   Would you divorce your wife for any other reason?   Yes / No

11.   In Jesus' statement, he described the position of the man who divorced his wife, what did he described?   True / False

12.   Jesus said whosoever divorce his wife except for sexual immorality, and marries another. What does it cause that person to do?   True / False

13.   Matthew 5:32: Jesus said that, whosoever shall put away his wife, saving for the cause of fornication, cause her to commit adultery   True / False

WORKSHEET: Concerning Marriage

TOPICS: Body, Freedom, Immorality, Marriage, Ministry, Morality, Prayer, Sex, Sin, Singleness, Slavery, Temptation, Unbelievers:

These are yes and no questions. Some maybe true or false. In either case, you are to answer one or both of them only if you are ask to do so; otherwise just answer one or check one or the other. You may also be asked to give the Scripture to support your answer if it is yes or no, or true or false, you will be ask to write it on the line that's given. You may use some of the words from the topics to draw answers from.

1. What is it to you that are good or bad about remaining single?

2. 1-Corinthian 7:10 asks that the wife should not depart from her husband   True / False

3. If the wife should depart from her husband should she remain unmarried?   True / False

4. A person who has gotten married by a notary, is that person from a biblical point a view is married spiritually as a person who has married not under the social way of living are the same spiritually? If your answer is yes, give the scripture that support your answer: Yes / No

5. A husband and wife as a divine ideal marriage is a lifelong bond that unites husband and wife in "one flesh" relationship?   True / False

6. Should a Christian go to a notary to become married? If your answer is yes, give scripture to support your answer: True / False

7. Does darkness have anything to do with light? If yes, give the scripture to support the answer: Yes / No

8. Why shouldn't a Christian get married by a notary? Explain: True / False

9. Should a minister become a notary and marry unbeliever outside the church?   Yes / No

10. Why shouldn't a minister who is a notary shouldn't marry outside the church? Is the notary outside the divine order spiritually?   Yes / No

11. Is a notary a part of the divine spiritual order of the church?   Yes / No

12. If a notary should want to marry someone in the house of Prayer, is that notary in a divine order according to the spiritual ethics?
If he or she is, give the scripture to support the answer:
If not write on the line (N/A)   Yes / No

13. Should a Christian go to the court house to become married?   True / False

14. A person who get married by a notary or by a notary in the court house be the same or have the same divine marriage as a person who is married in the House of Prayer by the pastor or a minister of the or a church?   True / False

WORKSHEET: Married by a Notary

1. Why shouldn't a Christian be married by a notary? Is it spiritual lawful for a Christian to be married by a notary?　　　　True / False

2. When a person is married by a notary is that person making divine views unto God and the views carrying the same values as a person who is married by the social settings of life?　　　　True / False

3. This same person that is getting marry by the notary, is he or she making the divine views as the person who is being married in saying let no man separate what God has joined together let no man separate these two people as husband and wife is carrying the same spiritual blessings of God as if he or she gotten married under the divine spiritual order of the house of prayer?
    If it is not true give the scripture that support your answer:　　　　True / False

4. Reasons that a Chastain shouldn't be married by a notary or unjust spiritual person: (Freedom), (Unbelievers),(Slavery), (Sin)　　　　True / False

5. Matthew 5:32: *But I say unto you, that whosoever shall put away his wife, saving for the cause of (fornication), cause her to commit (adultery :) and whosoever shall marry her that is divorced commit adultery.*　　　　True / False

6. Leviticus 21: 13: *When you marry a woman she is to have her virginity and so is the man is to be the same according to the biblical standard, and he shall take a wife in her (virginity)*　　　　True / False

7. (Acceptance), (Follow), (Marriage), (Priorities), (Privilege), and (Respect)

8. Why one should marry a woman who still has her virginity and so is the man. If you would look at this with a spiritual mind you can understand why Jesus said if a man put a way his wife he cause her to commit adultery. People today have already committed adultery both men and women before marriage. Woman are doing things to prevent having children which is not a part of the divine law of God's people. We need to go back to our first love and start all over again. This is pleasing in the eyes of God. What are your remarks?

150

WORKSHEET: A Justice of Peace and Notary

In this case I would like to talk about the two Christian people the Bible admonished to follow the Lord's teaching.

1. Under what circumstances may married partners derive each other's sexual needs? Is it a time when they consent within that time, that they may give themselves to fasting and prayer; and come together again, from a biblical point in ethically speaking — True / False

2. 1-Corinthians 7:5: Why is it important for a husband and wife not to deprive each other's sexual needs? According to the divine order of the biblical standards? — True / False

3. What instruction did the Bible give to the unmarried and widowed? — True / False

4. 1-Corinthians 7:8-9; and 7:15: To what has God called us?). — True / False

5. 1-Corinthians 7:8: I say therefore to the unmarried and widows, it is good for them if they abide even as I — True / False

6. 1-Corinthians 7:9: But if they cannot contain, let them marry — True / False

7. 1-Corinthians 7:9: What is more important than whether a person is married of single, what is more important to a person? God has distributed to every man, as he has called everyone, So, do you believe that every person should walk in that he has been called — Yes / No

8. Do you believe every man is called is circumcised by the word of? If your answer is yes, give Scripture to support — Yes / No

9. If a person is called being as such should he become circumcised? — Yes / No

10. If one is uncircumcised, should he be circumcised? — Yes / No

11. Does circumcision mean anything? — Yes / No

12. What's more important than circumcision? Explain:

13. Is circumcision the same as keeping the commandments of God? — Yes / No

14. Should a person abide in the same calling wherein he was called?   Yes / No

15. Should a minister of the divine order of the biblical standards become   Yes / No
    a notary? If you answer is no, explain:

16. Should a Christian of faith in God through Jesus Christ go to the   Yes / No
    justice of the peace for the people to be married as husband and wife?
    If your answer is yes give Scripture to support:

WORKSHEET: A Notary and the4 Justice of Peace

1. The justice of peace is a local magistrate who is authorize to marry a person who wish to become husband and wife

   True / False

2. Is a notary authorized to do the same

   Yes / No

3. In being the same, is either one that marry is authorize to give the divine blessings of God in marriage.
   If your answer is yes, give the Scripture that support the answer:

   Yes / No

4. If a local justice of peace should marry a person under what divine order is that person is joined together in marriage, is a civil order?

   Yes / No

5. If it isn't a divine order, if the marriage is not done in a divine order, is it a violation of that divine order? if your answer is no,, explain:

   Yes / No

6. When a notary marries a person with the authority of marrying, is to be said in the name of Jesus Christ our Lord and carrying the same views that would be carried out in a divine setting?
   If your answer is yes, give the Scripture to support the answer: , if the answer is no, than give some reflection on the reason:

   Yes / No

7. It has been said what God has ordained and joined together let no man put asunder

   True / False

8. Can the justice of peace be authorized with a divine biblical standard do this service under a divine order?
   If your answer is no, explain :

   Yes / No

9. Why shouldn't a person who believes by faith in God through the words of Jesus Christ:
   shouldn't be married by a justice of peace or a notary? Explain'

   Yes / No

10. Can the justice of peace or the notary that's of a social order become a divine social order perform a holy condition founded by God and be done at the will of man in marriage

    Yes / No

11. A Christian who believes in God through Jesus Christ, is their marriage union a holy condition founded by God and is not to be

    Yes / No

dissolved at the will of man

12. What factors tend to undermine a marriage and make a couple more susceptible to divorce?   True / False

13. Why is it that we aren't any longer twain, and being as one as it was ordained in the marriage, it was said by God what he has joined together, let no man put asunder?   True / False

14. Should we come together again in being reconciled together? Is this pleasing in the eyes of God?   True / False

Who were once enlightened and have tasted the heavenly gift (Hebrews 6:4-7)

If after they have escaped the pollution of the world (2-Peter 2:20-22).

If they shall fall away to renew them again unto repentance (Hebrews 6:6).

How much sorer punishment suppose you? (Hebrews 10:29).

Grieve not the holy spirit of God whereby you are sealed (Ephesians 4:30).

He who eats and drink unorthily eat and drink damnation unto himself (1-Corintians 11:20).

For this cause many are weak and sickly among you, and many are sleep. For if we would judge ourselves, we should not be judged (l-Corinthians 11:30-31)

If we confess our sins, he is faithful and just to forgive our sins, and to cleanse us from all unrighteousness (1-John 1:9).

Believers are to be dead to sin planted together in the likeness of his death (Romans 6:3-7).

Circumcised with the circumcision of Jesus Christ (Colossians 2:11-15).

What is the exceeding greatness of his power toward us who believe (Ephesians 1:19-20).

And being dead in your sin (Colossians 2:13).

Blotting out the handwriting of ordinance that was against us (Colossians 2:14).

Having abolished in his flesh the mity (Ephesians 2:15-16).

Knowing us out old man is crucified with him, that the body is dead to sin which is destroyed (Romans 6:6).

A WAY OF A RIGHTEOUSE LIFE

A POOR MAN'S PRAYER (PSALM 86:1-7)

Bow down your ear, Oh Lord, hears me: for I am poor and needy; Preserve my soul; for I am holy: Oh you are my God, Save your servant that trust in you. Be merciful unto me, Oh Lord: for I cry unto you daily. Rejoice the soul of your servant: for unto you, Oh Lord, do I lift up my soul. For you, Lord, are good, and ready to forgive, and plenteous in mercy unto all them who called upon you; Give ear, Oh Lord, unto my prayer, and attend to the voice of my supplication, in the day of my trouble I will call upon you: for You will answer me AMEN.

A PRAYER FOR STRENGTH

Most Holy And Merciful Father:
In the long hours of trying circumstance, When it seem that all strength is gone and Every fabric of our body is tested, help us to subject to trials and to understand, grant us the sufferance grace that will endure in the worst of times, and to remember that at the end of every burden or sorrow there is strength, faith, and wisdom. Father build in us a deeper knowledge that long suffering and endurance will grow best in the worst of times AMEN.